'EXCEL' in Business Analytics

William A. Young II | Andrew C. Goodnite

Kendall Hunt
publishing company

Cover image © Shutterstock.com

Kendall Hunt
publishing company

www.kendallhunt.com
Send all inquiries to:
4050 Westmark Drive
Dubuque, IA 52004-1840

ISBN 978-1-5249-4841-2

Published in the United States of America

CONTENTS

PREFACE

ABOUT THE BOOK

"Excel in Business Analytics" was not developed to be a traditional textbook used to teach business analytics in a traditional classroom setting. The objective of our textbook was to design a textbook that would support an active learning environment. For example, our primary goal of the textbook was to support educational videos that students watch before coming to an online or face-to-face "classroom." Before watching these videos, students are given Microsoft Excel files, which serve as starting files. While watching these videos, students are shown specific steps that they will need to complete in order to solve business-related problems using analytics. While completing these steps students are given instruction, and topics related to business analytics are discussed within the videos. However, in an active classroom, students are not always solving problems while watching educational videos. Educators may want to use their classroom time to solve additional problems, to work on homework assignments, or to conduct exams to assess whether students understand certain learning outcomes. In either case, students may want quick access to certain definitions, formulas, or other relevant information in order to solve problems. Regardless of how time is used in the classroom, our book was designed to acclimate readers to the importance and application of business analytics topics quickly and to provide information that is needed in order to solve problems within business using analytics quickly and easily.

The information and examples contained in the textbook could be used to support undergraduate and graduate college courses. Our textbook is focused on how to use Microsoft Excel to learn and to apply analytics in a business setting. We feel that there are several benefits to using Excel as our exclusive choice of software. However, the primary benefit is that Microsoft Excel is so widely available; it is likely that anyone who wants to learn business analytics has had some level of previous experience with the software, which reduces the barrier to learn. We do recognize that other, more specialized software exist for business analytics. However, our intention is to develop students who have either no previous or very limited knowledge of how to conduct quantitative studies using business analytics. Thus, we feel Microsoft Excel is a perfect choice for our intended audience.

This book is organized into four parts

- **DESCRIPTIVE STATISTICS:** The first three chapters provide the basic fundamental knowledge needed to work efficiently in Excel and defines the basic descriptive statistics needed to summarize data in tables and charts. No attempt has been made to cover every possible tool used to summarize data in Excel, this book focuses on the most common and most used techniques only.

- **INFERENTIAL STATISTICS:** Chapters 4 and 5 cover probability theory and hypothesis testing. Great care was taken to organize this material in a way that students could easily access the needed information quickly and easily.
- **PREDICTIVE ANALYTICS:** Chapters 6 and 7 cover regression and time series forecasting techniques.
- **PRESCRIPTIVE ANALYTICS:** Chapters 8 and 9 cover decision theory and optimization.

TO THE STUDENT

This text can serve as a reference book as you proceed through your business education program. In addition, as you move out into the workforce, it would be a good reference to have available to help you remember how to do important business analysis and analytics tasks in the workplace. The techniques presented in this text are used extensively in all areas of business including marketing, accounting, quality control, consumers, professional sports people, hospital administrators, educators, politicians, physicians, and so forth.

TO THE INSTRUCTOR

This text along with the associated videos, activities, in-class activities, homework, and exam questions has been designed to allow you to easily implement this course at your university.

The authors would like to thank you for considering our textbook for your course.

Sincerely,

William A. Young II, PhD
Andrew C. Goodnite, MBA & PMP

THE AUTHORS

Dr. William A. Young II is an Assistant Professor of Business Analytics in the Department of Analytics and Information Systems at Ohio University's College of Business. Professor Young was and continues to be a key contributor in establishing undergraduate and graduate programs in business analytics programs at Ohio University. His research and teaching interest lies within predictive and prescriptive analytics. Dr. Young earned his PhD in Mechanical and Systems Engineering at the Russ College of Engineering and Technology at Ohio University in 2010. In addition, Young also earned a Master and Bachelor of Science degrees in Electrical Engineering at Ohio University in 2005 and 2002, respectively. Professor Young has won teaching and researching awards for his contributions within business analytics.

Andrew Goodnite is an Analytics instructor at Ohio University. Professor Goodnite has dual master's degrees in Business Administration from Ohio University and Meteorology from the Air Force Institute of Technology as well as an bachelors degree in Atmospheric Sciences with minors in Mathematics and Physics from the University of Arizona. He is a retired Air Force officer who has also worked as a data analyst and project manager in corporate and higher education environments. His main teaching interest lies in teaching business analytics in an active classroom setting. He teaches the upper level Business Analytics course that is required for all College of Business undergraduate students and co-teaches with Dr. Young in the Analytics concentration courses of the MBA program.

CHAPTER 1

DESCRIPTIVE STATISTICS
Building Excel Skills

Microsoft Excel is perhaps the most important software program used in the workplace today. With that said, it would be wise for anyone that wants to work in business to learn how to use Excel effectively. Employers want employees to have a working understanding of how to use Excel effectively because it is important for a business to make business decisions that are supported by analyzing data.

It is very difficult to find someone that claims that they have no working knowledge of Excel. However, it has been our experience that almost everyone overestimates his or her ability to use Excel. Unfortunately, most people that say they know how to use Excel will not know the topics presented in this chapter. In this chapter, we will begin to explore best practices and other foundational skills one should have in order to use Excel effectively in the workplace. After completing this chapter and moving forward, you will have a skill set that is often lacking and highly sought after in the workplace. So let us begin our journey with a few definitions:

- An Excel file is called a Workbook.
- A Workbook contains many Worksheets.
- Worksheets are also referred to as Spreadsheets.
- Each column is identified by a unique letter (i.e., A, B, C, etc.).
- Each row is identified by a unique number (i.e., 1, 2, 3, etc.).
- The combination of column letter and row number gives a unique cell reference (i.e., A1).
- An array of cells is noted by the starting column and starting row, followed by a colon, and then the ending column and row (i.e., A1:B1, A1:C2, A1:D3, etc.).
- Cells typically contain numeric and text information that can be formatted in many ways.

Professional Formatting Guidance

As a business professional, the quality of our work is often judged by how well it is organized and presented. In the workplace, we create and share documents in both electronic and print versions. Since Microsoft Excel is often used to complete tasks, it only makes sense that we would want to be able to create the most professional-looking workbooks possible.

In order to create professional-looking and easy to understand documents, you should format your Excel spreadsheets using the following guidance. Most of the time, your instructors will not specify formatting in problem descriptions. However, they may deduct points if you do not follow good formatting practices. You may want to clarify this with your instructor, but it is our opinion that you should always strive to create a spreadsheet that is well organized and well formatted.

Currency

Currency should be formatted using either accounting or currency style with the $ sign and two places after the decimal point.

Very large numbers above $100,000 should be truncated to zero places after the decimal point. In addition, these numbers should have commas between every three digits.

TABLE 1 Various Formatting Settings for Currency

Currency Format	
Small Numbers	$1.23
Large Numbers	$123,456
Accounting Format	
Small Numbers	$1.23
Large Numbers	$123,456

Shortcut: The shortcut for Currency is "Control+Shift+$"

CAUTION: If there are no decimal places showing for a value in a cell, Excel rounds the value to the nearest whole number. This rounding will not affect mathematical calculations. In other words, calculations are not based on the number that is showing, but they are based on the value of the cell that may or may not be visible. However, if functions like ROUND, ROUNDUP, or ROUNDDOWN are used, they change the number that is stored in a cell and will affect mathematical calculations. Rounding can lead to significant calculation errors that can become quite large in some situations. Therefore, if you choose to use the rounding functions, there should be a specific reason why.

Percentages

Percentages should be formatted using the percentage style with the % sign and the number of places after the decimal point is situationally specific.

TABLE 2 Various Formatting Settings for Percentages

Percentages	
Acceptable	12%
Acceptable	12.3%
Acceptable	12.35%
Acceptable	12.346%
Unnecessary	12.345678%

Shortcut: The shortcut for Percentages is "Control+Shift+%".

Dates

Dates should be formatted as dates, using a consistent style that is desired .

Shortcut: A shortcut for Dates is "Control+Shift+#".

Borders

Borders should be placed around your data tables. See Table 2 for an example.

Column and Row Headers

Column and Row Headers should be clear and correctly identified. Bold font and/or filling column and row headers with a different color is a best practice. Headers and data should be centered in the columns. See Table 2 for an example.

Print Settings

Print settings should be correctly configured for any data table that may need to be printed.

Cell Protection

Cell protection should be correctly configured to protect formulas from accidental change.

Video Available: Watch the Chapter 1—Professional Formatting Video

Shortcut Keys

Microsoft Excel is a powerful software tool that is used on a daily basis by most business professionals. After you complete this course, your Excel skills will be at a far higher level than most of your co-workers. However, in order to make the most of the software, you should learn how to use a few key sequences on your keyboard (i.e., shortcuts).

Table 3 shows the most important shortcut keys available in Excel. If you commit these to memory, you can save yourself a lot of time in this course and afterward. By far, the most useful shortcut keys are the Control+Arrow and Control+Shift+Arrow keys. By using these keys, you can quickly move around large spreadsheets and select data as needed. Using these key sequences, formulas can be built very quickly.

TABLE 3 Essential Excel Shortcuts for Windows and MAC

Action	Windows Key Sequence	MAC Key Sequence
Save workbook	Control S	Command S
Undo last action	Control Z	Command Z
Cut selected cells	Control X	Command X
Copy selected cells	Control C	Command C
Paste selected cells	Control V	Command V
Redo last action	Control Y	Command Y
Display find dialog box	Control F	Command F
Display find and replace dialog box	Control H	Command H
Fill down from cell above	Control D	Control D
Fill right from cell left	Control R	Control R
Print	Control P	Command P
Display the Paste Special dialog box	Control Alt V	Control Command V
Quickly move around the worksheet	Control Arrow	Control Arrow
Go to previous worksheet	Control Page Up	Fn Control Up Arrow
Go to next worksheet	Control Page Down	Fn Control Down Arrow
Show formulas	Control ~	Control ~
Quickly select data in worksheet	Control Shift Arrow	Control Shift Arrow
Extend selected data	Shift Arrow	Shift Arrow
Delete rows or columns	Control -	Control -
Insert rows or columns	Control Shift +	Control I
Enter array formula	Control Shift Enter	Control Shift Return
Format selected data as a number with 2 significant digits	Control Shift !	Command Shift 1
Format selected data as time	Control Shift @	Command Shift 2
Format selected data as date	Control Shift #	Command Shift 3
Format selected data as currency	Control Shift $	Command Shift 4
Format selected data as percentages	Control Shift %	Command Shift 5
Open help	F1	Command /
Edit the active cell	F2	Control U
Toggle absolute and relative references	F4	Command T
Calculate worksheets	F9	Fn F9
Auto Sum selected cells	Alt =	Command Shift T
Start a new line in the same cell	Alt Enter	Control Option Return

Print the table above for a desktop reference.

Video Available: Watch the Chapter 1—Shortcut Key Video

Order of Operations

It is important to understand how Excel executes mathematical instructions in a spreadsheet. Luckily, Excel uses the same order of operations that are taught in our beginning level math courses.

TABLE 4 Correct Order of Operations

Order of Operations	
P	First, Do things in **P**arenthesis
E	Next, Do **E**xponents
M and D	Next **M**ultiply and **D**ivide
A and S	Finally, **A**dd and **S**ubtract
Please Excuse My Dear Aunt Sally	

All equivalent functions are to be executed left to right.

Video Available: Watch the Chapter 1—Order of Operations Video

Cell Referencing

One of the most important concepts to understand when creating formulas in Excel is called absolute, relative, and mixed cell referencing. By mastering this concept, you will be able to create one formula and copy it across and down a spreadsheet to quickly build tables of formulas without modification to each formula in the table. The position of a dollar sign ($) in a cell reference determines how the formula will behave when it is filled or copied right or down.

There are four possible settings for each cell reference

- With just the column letter and row number and no dollar signs, both the column and row are "relative"; this means that the column reference will increment as the formula is copied across the spreadsheet and the row reference will increment as the formula is copied down the spreadsheet.
    - **A1: both column and row are relative**
- With a dollar sign in front of both the column letter and the row number, both the column and row are "absolute"; this means neither the column or row reference will increment as the formula is copied across or down the spreadsheet.
    - **$A$1: both column and row are absolute**
- With a dollar sign in front of just the row number, the column reference will increment as the formula is copied across the spreadsheet but the row number will not increment as the formula is copied down.
    - **A$1: column is relative, row is absolute**

- With a dollar sign in front of just the column letter, the column reference will not increment as the formula is copied across the spreadsheet but the row number will increment as the formula is copied down.
  - **$A1: column is absolute, row is relative**
- You can toggle between the four different settings using the F4 key on a Windows PC or the Command T key on a MAC.

TABLE 5 Absolute, Relative, and Mixed Cell Reference Settings

Cell Referencing	
A1	both column and row are relative
$A$1	both column and row are absolute
A$1	column is relative, row is absolute
$A1	column is absolute, row is relative
Toggle settings using F4 (Cmd T on MAC)	

Video Available: Watch the Chapter 1—Cell Referencing Video

Date and Text Functions

While this section covers the basics of working with dates and text values, countless scenarios require manipulation of these types of data. If you encounter a situation not covered here, we recommend using Excel Help or search for help on the Internet in order to determine how to handle it. Dates are stored as integers (i.e., whole numbers), while times are stored as decimal fractions. For Windows Excel, Day 1 is January 1st, 1900, and the date increments by 1 each day from then. For MAC Excel, Day 1 is January 1st, 1904, and the date also increments by 1 each day from then. If you open a file created on one system using the other and the dates are off by 4 years and 1 day, it is a result of these different default-starting dates. You can change the defaults in the File, Options, Advanced area. The basic date functions we will cover are:

TABLE 6 Selected Date Functions

Date Functions	
Action	**Function**
To insert today's date use	=TODAY()
To insert today's date and time use	=NOW()
To pull the Day of the Month from a date column use	=DAY(cellref)
To pull the Month from a date column use	=MONTH(cellref) or =TEXT(cellref,"mmm")
To pull the Year from a date column use	=YEAR(cellref)
To compute years past use	=(TODAY()-DATE)/365

Video Available: Watch the Chapter 1—Dates and Text Function Video

Now that we covered some basic date functions, let us look at a couple useful text functions. First, to combine text fields use the AND symbol, it is called concatenate; there is also a concatenate function in Excel. If you want to pull out a portion of the characters from a text field, use the LEFT, RIGHT, or MID functions but please note that numerical values pulled out of a text string are still considered text values in Excel. You will need to use the VALUE function to convert them to numbers. You can check to see how a value is stored in Excel by using the TYPE function. If TYPE returns a 1, then the value is a number. If TYPE returns a 2, the value is text.

It should be noted that anytime you put double quotes around a number (i.e., "1"), Excel will treat the cell as a text value. Thus, you should never put double quotes around numbers if you intend to use the value of the cell to do mathematical calculations or comparisons.

TABLE 7 Selected Text Functions

Text Functions	
Action	**Function**
To combine text columns use	= cellref&cellref
To pull out characters from the left side of a text field use	= LEFT(cellref,#char)
To pull out characters from the right side of a text field use	= RIGHT(cellref,#char)
To pull out characters from the middle of a text field use	= MID(cellref,startnum,numchars)
Value pulled out will be a text value even if it looks like a number	
Convert a text number to a real number use	=VALUE(cellref)
To identify the type of data in a cell use	=TYPE 1= number, 2=text

Video Available: Watch the Chapter 1—Dates and Text Function Video

SUMPRODUCT Function

The SUMPRODUCT function is a very useful function in Business Analytics because it can be used to find answers to common business calculations quickly such as Production Costs, Shipping Costs, and Revenue. Keep in mind the following aspects of the SUMPRODUCT formula.

- The SUMPRODUCT function can be used to solve equations of the type: $=B_1*X_1+B_2*B_2+B_3*X_3$ and so on.
- It is used for expense and revenue equations like Production Costs, which is the number of items produced times the cost to produce each item.
- It is also used for Shipping Cost which is the number of items shipped times the cost to ship each item.
- Another example is revenue, which is a number of items sold times the sales price for each item.
- The structure is SUMPRODUCT(range1,range2).
- Both ranges need to be the same size and shape.

- Both ranges need to be structured in the same manner.

TABLE 8 SUMPRODUCT Example

	A	B	C	D	E
1	**Number of Items to Ship**				
2		**Destination**			
3	**Source**	Chicago IL	St. Louis MO	Atlanta GA	Dallas TX
4	Athens OH	16	28	44	52
5	Parkersburg WV	12	34	26	58
6					
7	**Cost to Ship Each Item**				
8		**Destination**			
9	**Source**	Chicago IL	St. Louis MO	Atlanta GA	Dallas TX
10	Athens OH	$34.99	$35.01	$38.28	$46.12
11	Parkersburg WV	$36.55	$35.99	$35.21	$43.34
12					
13	Total Shipping Cost:	$10,714.12	without SUMPRODUCT		
14	=B4*B10+C4*C10+D4*D10+E4*E10+B5*B11+C5*C11+D5*D11+E5*E11				
15					
16	Total Shipping Cost:	$10,714.12	with SUMPRODUCT		
17	=SUMPRODUCT(B4:E5,B10:E11)				

You should know that the SUMPRODUCT is a very useful formula for Predictive and Prescriptive Analytics in Excel. In Predictive Analytics, linear equations of the form of $A+B_1*X_1+B_2*B_2+B_3*X_3$ are often the basis for mathematical modeling techniques such as multiple linear regression, logistic regression, discriminate analysis, and artificial neural networks. In Prescriptive Analytics, optimization models often use a linear combination of coefficients and other numeric values in order to calculate constraint parameters and objective functions.

TRANSPOSE Function

As noted, one requirement to use the SUMPRODUCT formula is that your ranges must be of the same size. In other words, if you select the first range and it has M number of rows and N columns, then the second range of data must have M number of rows and N columns. If you have a situation where one range of data has M rows and N columns, and the second range N rows and M columns (i.e., the opposite), then we can use the TRANSPOSE function to make SUMPRODUCT work correctly. However, it must be entered in a very specific way.

TRANSPOSE is a function that can be used to change the dimensions of an array. For example, if a range is selected as the parameter of a TRANSPOSE function and this range had M number of rows and N columns, the TRANSPOSE function would create an array that consisted of N number of rows and M number of columns. If you are in a situation where you need to use the TRANSPOSE function, please remember that it needs to be entered by using the Control+Shift+Enter keyboard sequence.

TABLE 9 SUMPRODUCT With TRANSPOSE Example

	A	B	C	D	E
1	**Number of Items to Ship**				
2		**Destination**			
3	**Source**	Chicago IL	St. Louis MO	Atlanta GA	Dallas TX
4	Athens OH	16	28	44	52
5	Parkersburg WV	12	34	26	58
6					
7		**Cost to Ship Each Item**			
8			**Source**		
9		**Destination**	Athens OH	Parkersburg WV	
10		Chicago IL	$34.99	$36.55	
11		St. Louis MO	$35.01	$35.99	
12		Atlanta GA	$38.28	$35.21	
13		Dallas TX	$46.12	$43.34	
14					
15	Total Shipping Cost:	$10,714.12	with SUMPRODUCT and TRANSPOSE		
16	{=SUMPRODUCT(B4:E5,TRANSPOSE(C10,D13))}				
17	This is an array function and must be entered using **"Control Shift Enter"** in B15				

Video Available: Watch the Chapter 1—SUMPRODUCT Video

IF Statements

IF statements play an extremely important role when it comes to building dynamic spreadsheets. They play an important role in Business Analytics because we often need to make logical comparisons between two or more values and then perform some sort of mathematical operation given the result of the comparisons. From a Predictive Analytics perspective, we often need to encode text values into numerical, binary values. This process is called dummy variable creation. When writing logical statements it is important to understand the following logical operators.

TABLE 10 Logical Operators

Logic	Operator
Equal to	=
Greater than	>
Less than	<
Greater than or equal to	>=
Less than or equal to	<=
Not equal to	<>

IF Statements and Binary Encoding

IF statements allow you to make logical comparisons between two or more values. These comparisons can either be between qualitative attribute, or between two quantitative values. As noted, IF statements can be used in order to create binary encodings of text attributes. Binary encoding simply means that we are going to transform text attributes into numeric ones. For example, if we have a column of text attributes, we will create an additional column where a 1 might represent the result of an IF statement's TRUE response and a 0 might represent an IF statement's FALSE response. Below, you will see a list of things to consider when developing an IF statement.

- Answers questions where logical comparisons are required.
- Can be used in a stand-alone mode or as part of a formula.
- IF statements that assign a value of 1 for TRUE and a value of 0 for FALSE are called Binary Encoding.
- =IF(logical_test,value_if_true,value_if_false).
- Logical_test is any value or expression that can be evaluated to TRUE or FALSE.
- Value_if_true is the value you wish to be assigned if the logical test returns TRUE.
- Value_if_false is the value you wish to be assigned if the logical test returns FALSE.
- Always put quotes around text values but do not put quotes around numbers or cell references.

TABLE 11 IF Statement With Binary Encoding Example

	A	B	C	D
1	**Name**	**Bachelor's Degree**	**Bachelor's Degree Encoded Binary Example**	**Binary IF Statement Structure**
2	John Smith	Yes	1	=IF(B2="Yes",1,0)
3	James Adams	No	0	=IF(B3="Yes",1,0)
4	Bill Williams	Yes	1	=IF(B4="Yes",1,0)
5	Cindy Jones	No	0	=IF(B5="Yes",1,0)

Video Available: Watch the Chapter 1—If Statements Video

Nested IF Statements

Users can state what result they would like to perform if an IF statement returns a TRUE or a FALSE result of a logical comparison. An IF statement is to be nested if an additional IF is used in the FALSE position of another IF statement. IF statements allow us to compare multiple comparisons and take the correct course of action provided whether a specific logical statement is TRUE or FALSE. In general, once an IF statement returns a TRUE result, some sort of value is displayed and the remaining logical comparisons are ignored. Here are some things to keep in mind when writing nested IF statements.

- Answers questions where logical comparisons of more than one variable are required and ANY of the conditions can be TRUE.
- IF OR statement or a Nested IF can be used interchangeably in some situations.
- Can be used in a stand-alone mode or as part of a formula.
- =IF(logical1,value_if_true, IF(logical2,value_if_true, value_if_false)).
- Logical1 is any value or expression that can be evaluated to TRUE or FALSE.

- Logical2 is the next value or expression to be evaluated to TRUE or FALSE.
- More logical statements can be added by adding another IF nest in place of the value_if_false.
- Value_if_true is the value you wish to be assigned if the logical test returns TRUE.
- Value_if_false is the value you wish to be assigned if the logical test returns FALSE.
- Always put quotes around text values but do not put quotes around numbers or cell references.

TABLE 12 NESTED IF Statement Example

	A	B	C
1	**Reference Table: Pay Raise Criteria**		
2	**Rating**	**Raise Percentage**	
3	1	0%	
4	2	1%	
5	3	2%	
6	4	3%	
7			
8	**Name**	**Rating**	**Pay Raise Nested IF Example**
9	John Smith	2	1.0%
10	James Adams	1	0.0%
11	Bill Williams	4	3.0%
12	Cindy Jones	3	2.0%
13	Nested IF Statement Structure (formula from cell C9)		
14	=IF(B9=$A$3,$B$3,IF(B9=$A$4,$B$4,IF(B9=$A$5,$B$5,IF(B9=$A$6,$B$6,0))))		

Video Available: Watch the Chapter 1—IF Statements Video

IF AND Statements

An AND statement will pass a logical TRUE if all of the logical statements inside of the AND statement are TRUE. An AND statement can be used in conjunction with an IF statement and at times can reduce the excessive need for complicated nested IF statements. Observe the following notes:

- Answers questions where logical comparisons of more than one variable are required and all conditions must be TRUE.
- Can be used in a stand-alone mode or as part of a formula.
- =IF(AND(logical1,logical2),value_if_true, value_if_false).
- Logical1 is any value or expression that can be evaluated to TRUE or FALSE.
- Logical2 is the next value or expression to be evaluated to TRUE or FALSE.
- More logical statements can be added by adding another comma and the next logical inside the AND parenthesis.
- Value_if_true is the value you wish to be assigned if the logical test returns TRUE.
- Value_if_false is the value you wish to be assigned if the logical test returns FALSE.
- Always put quotes around text values but do not put quotes around numbers or cell references.

TABLE 13 IF AND Statement Example

	A	B	C	D
1	**Name**	**Years With Company**	**Salary**	**Example: Years > 15 AND Salary <= $35000**
2	John Smith	16	$32,323	TRUE
3	James Adams	6	$32,545	FALSE
4	Bill Williams	31	$35,000	TRUE
5	Cindy Jones	18	$72,732	FALSE
6	IF AND Statement Structure (formula from cell D2)			
7	=IF(AND(B2>15,C2<=35000),TRUE,FALSE)			

Video Available: Watch the Chapter 1—IF Statements Video

IF OR Statements

An OR statement will pass a logical TRUE if at least one of the logical statements inside of the OR statement is TRUE. An OR statement can be used in conjunction with an IF statement and at times can reduce the excessive need for complicated nested IF statements. Consider the following:

- Answers questions where logical comparisons of more than one variable are required and ANY of the conditions can be TRUE.
- Can be used in a stand-alone mode or as part of a formula.
- =IF(OR(logical1,logical2),value_if_true, value_if_false).
- Logical1 is any value or expression that can be evaluated to TRUE or FALSE.
- Logical2 is the next value or expression to be evaluated to TRUE or FALSE.
- More logical statements can be added by adding another comma and the next logical inside the OR parenthesis.
- Value_if_true is the value you wish to be assigned if the logical test returns TRUE.
- Value_if_false is the value you wish to be assigned if the logical test returns FALSE.
- Always put quotes around text values but do not put quotes around numbers or cell references.

TABLE 14 IF OR Statement Example

	A	B	C	D
1	**Name**	**Years With Company**	**Bachelor's Degree**	**Example: If Years <= 5 OR Bachelors = Yes**
2	John Smith	16	Yes	TRUE
3	James Adams	6	No	FALSE
4	Bill Williams	31	Yes	TRUE
5	Cindy Jones	18	No	FALSE
6	IF OR Statement Structure (formula from cell D2)			
7	=IF(OR(B2<=5,C2="Yes"),TRUE,FALSE)			

Video Available: Watch the Chapter 1—IF Statements Video

IF AND OR and IF OR AND Statements

Though it might be rare, a combination of AND OR and OR AND statements can be used together to produce complex logical comparisons. Using this combination can help define just about any conceivable set of logical comparisons that you may want. Consider the following general expressions:

- IF AND OR example: =IF(AND(OR(logical1, logical2),OR(logical1,logical2)), 1,0)
- IF OR AND example: =IF(OR(AND(logical1, logical2),AND(logical1,logical2)), 1,0)

TABLE 15 IF AND OR and IF OR AND Statements Example

	A	B	C	D	E
1	**Name**	**Rating**	**Years With Company**	**IF AND OR if Rating = 4 or Years > 6 AND Rating = 3 or Years > 3**	**IF OR AND if Rating = 4 and Years > 6 OR Rating = 3 and Years > 3**
2	John Smith	2	16	TRUE	FALSE
3	James Adams	1	6	FALSE	FALSE
4	Bill Williams	4	31	TRUE	TRUE
5	Cindy Jones	3	18	TRUE	TRUE
6	IF AND OR Statement Structure (formula from cell D2)				
7	=IF(AND(OR(B2=4,C2>6),OR(B2=3,C2>3)),TRUE,FALSE)				
8					
9	IF AND OR Statement Structure (formula from cell E2)				
10	=IF(OR(AND(B2=4,C2>6),AND(B2=3,C2>3)),TRUE,FALSE)				

Video Available: Watch the Chapter 1—IF Statements Video

Conditional Formatting

Conditional formatting can be used to bring your spreadsheets to life. Conditional formatting works in a dynamic manner. Excel has a number of built-in conditional formatting rules that you can easily select from Excel's Home Ribbon. You can also define custom formulas in order to control the formatting of cells in a dynamic manner. If you build formulas to control the conditional formatting, you will likely use the same logical operators discussed previously (i.e., AND and OR).

TABLE 16 Conditional Formatting With User Defined Rule Example

	A	B	C	D
1	**Name**	**Years With Company**	**Salary**	**Example: Years > 15 AND Salary <= $35000**
2	John Smith	16	$32,323	TRUE
3	James Adams	6	$32,545	FALSE
4	Bill Williams	31	$35,000	TRUE
5	Cindy Jones	18	$72,732	FALSE
6	Conditional Formatting Statement Structure (User Defined Rule)			
7	=AND($B2>15,$C2<=35000)			

In Table 16, employees with more than 15 years with the company and a salary less than $35,000 are conditionally formatted using a Yellow Fill.

Video Available: Watch the Chapter 1—Conditional Formatting Video

INDEX and MATCH Functions

Whether you work in marketing, accounting, sales, human resources, finance, or any other business area, a large part of your job will most likely consist of searching through large data sets and pulling out information on specific records. Learning to use the INDEX and VLOOKUP functions will give you the ability to do this very quickly. In order to pull information from selected data sets, we need to have at least one data element that has a unique value for each record. Examples are an employee number, customer number, serial number, social security number, and so on. In fact, the reason these numbers are assigned is to allow for matching up data tables across databases and spreadsheets. The set of unique values is called a Key field in relational databases.

In Excel, we can use either the INDEX or VLOOKUP function together with the MATCH function to perform this task. INDEX and VLOOKUP return the contents of a cell and the MATCH function is used to find the correct cell.

- INDEX functions return the contents of a cell given the correct row and column in a table (2D array) of data.
- MATCH functions return the correct row and column given a lookup value in a column or row (1D array) of data.
  - Used to pull selected data out of large spreadsheets, requires a unique identifier to use as a lookup value
- =INDEX(array,row,column)
  - Array—the 2D table of data that contains the information you need to lookup
  - Row—the row number of the table of data containing the information you are looking for
  - Column—the column number of the table of data containing the information you are looking for
  - use a MATCH function to find the correct row and column numbers
- =MATCH(lookup_value,lookup-array,match_type)
  - **Row MATCH**
    - lookup_value is the unique identifier that you are using to find the correct record (employee #, customer ID, etc.)
    - lookup_array is the column in the table of data that has the unique identifier
    - match_type—use 0 for exact matches
    - match_type—use 1 for approximate matches where identifier column is sorted in ascending order (this is the default)
    - match_type—use -1 for approximate matches where identifier column is sorted in descending order
  - **Column MATCH**
    - lookup_value is the column heading that matches the column heading in the data table for the column that has the data you want to pull out
    - lookup_array is the row in the data table that has the column headers listed
    - match_type—use 0 for exact matches
    - This column match can be replaced with a number if you want to hard-code in the correct column to return
- Ex:=INDEX($A$32:$G$45,MATCH($B49,$D$32:$D$45,0),MATCH(C$48,$A$32:$G$32,0))

TABLE 17 INDEX MATCH MATCH Statement Example

	A	B	C
1		**Example Data Set**	
2	**Employee Number**	**Name**	**Years With Company**
3	EMP0005043	John Smith	16
4	EMP0001142	Brandie Lollis	41
5	EMP0004101	Bill Williams	31
6	EMP0002807	James Adams	6
7	EMP0009207	Ahmad Roper	26
8	EMP0001907	Jamal Snowball	56
9	EMP0009475	Cindy Jones	18
10			
11		**INDEX MATCH MATCH Example**	
12	**Employee Number**	**Name**	**Years With Company**
13	EMP0005043	John Smith	16
14	EMP0002807	James Adams	6
15	EMP0009475	Cindy Jones	18
16		INDEX Statement Structure (formula from cell C13)	
17		=INDEX($A$2:$C$9,MATCH($A13,$A$2:$A$9,0),MATCH(C$12,$A$2:$C$2,0))	

Learning how to use a combination of INDEX and MATCH can be challenging. However, it is perhaps the most powerful combination of functions that you will use in Excel.

Video Available: Watch the Chapter 1—INDEX MATCH Video

VLOOKUP Function

VLOOKUP function returns the contents of a cell given the correct row and column in a table (2D array) of data.

- MATCH functions return the correct column given a lookup value in a row (1D array) of data
- Used to pull selected data out of large spreadsheets, required a unique identifier to use as a lookup value
- =VLOOKUP(lookup_value,table_array, column_index_number,range_lookup)
  - lookup_value is the unique identifier that you are using to find the correct record (employee #, customer ID, etc.)
  - table_array is the 2D table of data that contains the information you need to lookup
  - column_index_number is the column in the data table that has the data you want to pull out, can be hard-coded or found using MATCH

* range_lookup—use FALSE for exact matches and TRUE for approximate matches where identifier column is sorted in ascending order (TRUE is the default)
* ex: =VLOOKUP($J2,$A$1:$G$100,MATCH (K$1,$A$1:$G$1,0),FALSE)

TABLE 18 VLOOKUP MATCH Statement Example

	A	B	C
1		Example Data Set	
2	Employee Number	Name	Years With Company
3	EMP0005043	John Smith	16
4	EMP0001142	Brandie Lollis	41
5	EMP0004101	Bill Williams	31
6	EMP0002807	James Adams	6
7	EMP0009207	Ahmad Roper	26
8	EMP0001907	Jamal Snowball	56
9	EMP0009475	Cindy Jones	18
10			
11		VLOOKUP MATCH Example	
12	Employee Number	Name	Years With Company
13	EMP0005043	John Smith	16
14	EMP0002807	James Adams	6
15	EMP0009475	Cindy Jones	18
16		VLOOKUP Statement Structure (formula from cell C13)	
17		=VLOOKUP($A13,$A$2:$C$9,MATCH(C$12,$A$2:$C$2,0),FALSE)	

VLOOKUP is a very popular formula in business; however, it is wise to understand that it has limitations that a combination of INDEX and MATCH can overcome.

Video Available: Watch the Chapter 1—INDEX MATCH Video

CHAPTER 2

DESCRIPTIVE STATISTICS
Summarizing Data

In Chapter 1, we learned how to use some of Excel's functions like SUM, SUMPRODUCT, IF, INDEX, and MATCH. In this chapter, we will explore Excel's descriptive statistics functions in order to summarize data. Using Excel, we can quickly, and easily, create summary tables and charts using descriptive statistics. What is a descriptive statistic? Simply put, descriptive statistics are measurements derived from the data that we are trying to summarize that allow us to describe certain characteristics about data and their associated distributions. Common descriptive statistics include the count, mean, median, mode, minimum, maximum, standard deviation, and variance. Descriptive statistics can help answer the following questions:

- How many data points were used to summarize the data (i.e., the COUNT)?
- What is the center of the data that I am summarizing (i.e., AVERAGE, MEDIAN, and MODE)?
- What is the minimum of the data that I am summarizing (i.e., MIN)?
- What is the maximum of the data that I am summarizing (i.e., MAX)?
- What is the dispersion of the data that I am summarizing (i.e., STDEV.S or VAR.S)?

The AVERAGE function in Excel calculates the mean of the data that is selected. However, technically speaking, the mean, median, and mode, are all forms of averages which try to explain the center of the data's distribution.

Basic descriptive statistics are not always sufficient in order to summarize the data that we are trying to understand. In order to understand the data that we are summarizing better, we often need to calculate conditional descriptive statistics. What are conditional descriptive statistics? Essentially, we are talking about the same descriptive statistics that we have previously described. However, the word conditional implies that a descriptive statistic is calculated based on a subset of our original data. In other words, the descriptive statistic is calculated for a very particular set of data that we are trying to summarize. For example, assume we have a spreadsheet that includes the names of a company's employees and each employee's gender and salary. We may want to calculate the company's mean salary. If that were the case, we would simply calculate the mean of all of the salaries regardless of whether the employees were male or female. However, we might also want to calculate the conditional descriptive statistics of the mean salary for males and the mean salary for females. In this case, the condition, or what is referred to as the criteria of the descriptive statistic, would be the employee's gender. In other words, let us calculate the average salary if the employee identifies as a particular gender.

Before we look at how to compute conditional descriptive statistics, it is important to review the concepts related to data types and measurement scales. This is important because they will play a role in the criteria we use to calculate a conditional descriptive statistic.

Types of Data and Measurement Scales

TABLE 1 Qualitative Data vs. Quantitative Data

Qualitative Data	Quantitative Data
Qualitative data is non-numeric data	Quantitative data is numeric data
Examples: Political affiliation, gender, state of birth, method of payment, etc.	Examples: Price, age, salary, profit, opening deposit, account balance, exam scores, etc.

TABLE 2 Discrete Data vs. Continuous Data

Discrete Data	Continuous Data
Discrete variables can only take on integer values between its minimum and maximum value.	Continuous variables can take on any value between its minimum and maximum value.
Examples: number of items sold, built, shipped, etc.	Examples: Salary, account balance, profit, etc.

In terms of measurement scales, there are four levels. Consider the following definitions and examples.

1. **Nominal Scale**: The nominal scale is the lowest level of measurement. Nominal values are usually qualitative (i.e., text) and are assigned a discrete numeric value (i.e., 1, 2, 3, etc.). For example, assume we are designing a survey where we would like the respondent to indicate their gender. We might assign Female with a numeric response of 1, Male with a numeric response of 2, Other as a numeric value of 3. Nominal values do not have a quantitative meaning other than to represent the qualitative information numerically. For these types of values, there is no meaning between the numeric value and the order. In other words, a value of 2 is not twice as meaningful as a 1 nor does it imply that 2 is better than 1. Based on this example, we would say that nominal values do not have order and there is not a particular scale in which they are measured. Since nominal values are typically related to qualitative data, we cannot calculate very many descriptive statistics for this type of data. In this case, we are often limited to calculating the frequency of how many times each nominal value appeared

in the data set that we are trying to summarize. However, nominal values are very useful in determining the criteria for a conditional descriptive statistic.

In Latin, nominal means name. Thus, when you hear the word nominal, you should ask yourself, does the numeric value (i.e., 1) simply represent a qualitative attribute (i.e., text)?

2. **Ordinal Scale**: The ordinal scale is the next to lowest level of measurement. Ordinal values imply that the data is being used to distinguish order among the data points. For example, school rank would be an example of an ordinal value. Thus, we might associate a Freshman as a 1, a Sophomore as a 2, a Junior as a 3, and a Senior as a 4. In this case, discrete numbers are being used to represent the qualitative name, much like a nominal value. However, there is a big difference between nominal and ordinal values. Namely, ordinal values are based on integer values that imply order in the values that they are representing. For example, a Senior, which could be represented by a 4, is a grade level above a Junior, which could be represented by a 3. This implied order does not occur with nominal values. In other words, in the previous example related to nominal values, any numeric value could have represented any of the survey response options.

When you hear the word ordinal, you ask yourself, is there some sort of meaning related to the order of the numeric values that are used to represent a qualitative attribute?

3. **Interval Scale**: The interval scale is the third highest level of measure. Interval measurements are unlike nominal and ordinal values. Interval values are not simply numeric representations of qualitative information. In this case, interval values truly represent a numeric measurement based on some sort of defined measurement scale. For example, think about a situation where we are measuring temperature on a thermometer, which uses a Fahrenheit scale. Interval scales have equal measurements between specified points (i.e., 80°F and 81°F). For example, the thermometer is marked with numeric values that indicate the temperature. The distance between 80°F and 100°F is the same as the distance between 0°F and 20°F. However, in this case, it is important to know that 0°F is not an absolute or true zero point. In other words, it can get colder than 0°F. Thus, we can have negative values on this particular scale. Given that there is no absolute zero point of this scale, we cannot call it the highest level of measure.

When you hear the word interval, you should ask yourself if there is an absolute 0 point. If there is, then it is not an interval value. If there is not, then it must be a ratio level of measurement.

4. **Ratio Scale**: Ratio scale is the highest level of measurement. This measurement is similar to the interval scale except these measurements have an absolute or true zero point. For example, consider that we are measuring distances with a tape measure. The tape measure satisfies the requirements of an equal scale. In other words, there is an equal scale between 1 inch and 2 inches and 2 inches to 3 inches. Furthermore, each increment on this scale is based on the same interval. These measurements are of course ordered, which means that 1 inch is less than 2 inches. However, we can also say that 1 inch is exactly 1 inch less than 2 inches. Thus, the

attribute is ordinal and interval. However, based on this example, the attribute is also ratio because an absolute zero point exists. In other words, we cannot have negative values, or in this case, negative inches. For ratio values, we can calculate all descriptive statistics.

When you hear the word ratio, you should ask yourself if there is an absolute 0 point. If there is, then it is an ratio value. If there is not, then it must be an interval level of measurement providing that the level of measurement is at least ordinal.

Video Available: Watch the Chapter 2—Measurement Scales Video

Counting the Number of Occurrences

The count is the number of entries in a range or array that meet a given set of conditions. There are many counting formulas in Excel. Please review the functions listed below in order to understand their differences.

Excel Functions for Counting

=COUNT(range)—Counts the number of cells that contain numbers in the given range
=COUNTA(range)—Counts the number of cells that contain any value in the given range
=COUNTBLANK(range)—Counts the number of cells that are blank in the given range
=COUNTIFS(criteria_range1,criteria1, criteria_range2,criteria2]...)

- Counts the number of cells that contain values that meet the associated criteria.
- criteria_range1—Required. The first range in which to evaluate the associated criteria.
- criteria1—Required. The criteria in the form of a number, expression, cell reference, or text that define which cells will be counted. For example, criteria can be expressed as 32, ">32", B4, "apples," or "32."
- criteria_range2, criteria2, ... Optional. Additional ranges and their associated criteria. Up to 127 range/criteria pairs are allowed.

TABLE 3 Counting Functions Example

	A	B	C
1	**New Accounts Opened at New Harbor Bank**		
2	**Customer ID**	**Customer Service Rep**	**Opening Deposit**
3	CID1552	Brian Jones	$3,010
4	CID1636	Cindy Rogers	$221
5	CID1574	Cindy Rogers	$2,913
6	CID1976	Cindy Rogers	$3,870
7	CID1963	Brian Jones	$940
8	CID1803	Brian Jones	N/A
9	CID1619	Cindy Rogers	$4,664
10	CID1837	Cindy Rogers	
11	CID1506	Brian Jones	$4,035
12			
13	**Total Accounts Opened With Valid Opening Deposits**		7
14	COUNT Function Structure (from cell C13)		=COUNT(C3:C11)
15	Note: This function only counts cells with numeric values		
16			
17	**Total Number of Accounts Opened**		8
18	COUNTA Function Structure (from cell C17)		=COUNTA(C3:C11)
19	Note: This function doesn't count cells that are blank		
20			
21	**Total Number of Accounts Opened**		1
22	COUNTBLANK Function Structure (from cell C21)		=COUNTBLANK(C3:C11)
23	Note: This function only counts cells that are blank		
24			
25	**COUNTIFS Function Example**		
26	**Customer Service Rep**	**Number Accounts Opened**	
27	Brian Jones	4	
28	Cindy Rogers	5	
29	COUNTIFS Function Structure (from cell B27)		
30	=COUNTIFS($B$3:$B$11,A27)		

Older versions of Excel may not have a COUNTIFS function. If COUNTIFS is not available on your version of Excel, you should have the COUNTIF function available. This function is similar to COUNTIFS; however, it only allows one criteria to be entered. Even if you only have one criteria, it is considered best practice if you use a COUNTIFS instead of COUNTIF.

Video Available: Watch the Chapter 2—Counting Functions Video

Counting With Continuous Criteria

The COUNTIFS function, as well as the rest of the conditional descriptive statistics that we will introduce in this chapter, allows us to calculate the statistic based on a set of continuous criteria. A set of continuous criteria is a set of ranges with each range having a minimum value and a maximum value. For example, the first range may be from 0 to 999, the next range may be from 1000 to 1999, and so forth. To calculate the conditional descriptive statistic for a given range, we need to use the correct function with two criteria. The following example shows the COUNTIFS function given a set of continuous criteria. This type of criteria configuration can be applied to the other conditional descriptive statistics that we will cover later in this chapter.

TABLE 4 Continuous Criteria Example

	A	B	C
1	**New Accounts Opened at New Harbor Bank**		
2	**Customer ID**	**Customer Service Rep**	**Opening Deposit**
3	CID1552	Brian Jones	$3,010
4	CID1636	Cindy Rogers	$221
5	CID1574	Cindy Rogers	$2,913
6	CID1976	Cindy Rogers	$3,870
7	CID1963	Brian Jones	$940
8	CID1803	Brian Jones	N/A
9	CID1619	Cindy Rogers	$4,664
10	CID1837	Cindy Rogers	
11	CID1506	Brian Jones	$4,035
12			
13	**COUNTIFS With Continuous Criteria Example—Hard-coded**		
14	**Range**		**Number Accounts Opened**
15	$0 up to $2500		2
16	$2500 up to $5000		5
17	COUNTIFS Function Structure (from cell C15)		
18	=COUNTIFS($C$3:$C$11,”>=0”,$C$3:$C$11,”<2500”)		
19			
20	**COUNTIFS With Continuous Criteria Example–Dynamic References**		
21	**Lower Bound**	**Upper Bound**	**Number Accounts Opened**
22	$0	$2,500	2
23	$2,500	$5,000	5
24	COUNTIFS Function Structure (from cell C22)		
25	=COUNTIFS($C$3:$C$11,”>=”&A22,$C$3:$C$11,”<”&B22)		

Video Available: Watch the Chapter 2—Counting Functions Video

Summing the Number of Occurrences

The sum is the amount obtained as a result of adding numbers in a given range. There are just a few summing functions in Excel. Please see the short list below.

Excel Functions for Summing Data

=SUM(range)—Adds up the values in the cells in the given range
=SUMIFS(sum_range,criteria_range1,criteria1,[criteria_range2, criteria2]...)

- Adds up the values in the sum_range given the criteria is met.
- sum_range—Required. The range of cells to sum.
- criteria_range1—Required. The first range in which to evaluate the associated criteria.
- criteria1—Required. The criteria in the form of a number, expression, cell reference, or text that define which cells will be counted. For example, criteria can be expressed as 32, ">32", B4, "apples", or "32".
- criteria_range2, criteria2, ... Optional. Additional ranges and their associated criteria. Up to 127 range/criteria pairs are allowed.

TABLE 5 SUM Functions Example

	A	B	C
1	New Accounts Opened at New Harbor Bank		
2	Customer ID	Customer Service Rep	Opening Deposit
3	CID1552	Brian Jones	$3,010
4	CID1636	Cindy Rogers	$221
5	CID1574	Cindy Rogers	$2,913
6	CID1976	Cindy Rogers	$3,870
7	CID1963	Brian Jones	$940
8	CID1803	Brian Jones	N/A
9	CID1619	Cindy Rogers	$4,664
10	CID1837	Cindy Rogers	
11	CID1506	Brian Jones	$4,035
12			
13	Total Amount of Opening Deposits		$19,653
14	SUM Function Structure (from cell C13)		=SUM(C3:C11)
15			
16	SUMIFS Function Example		
17	Customer Service Rep	Total Amount of Opening Deposits	
18	Brian Jones	$7,985	
19	Cindy Rogers	$11,668	
20	SUMIFS Function Structure (from cell B18)		
21	=SUMIFS($C$3:$C$11,$B$3:$B$11,A18)		

The SUM and SUMIFS functions ignore blank and non-numeric cells.

Shortcut: The shortcut to SUM a range of data is "Alt =". This shortcut can be entered underneath or beside a row of data that you want to SUM. In addition, you can simply highlight the data that you want to SUM and you can use "ALT =" to SUM the data you have highlighted.

Video Available: Watch the Chapter 2—Summing Functions Video

Extreme Values

Often we need to find the extreme values in a set of data. Excel gives us many different ways to find these values. We will discuss the following methods.

Excel Functions

=MIN(range)—returns the minimum value in a given range
=MAX(range)—returns the maximum value in a given range
=SMALL(range,k)—returns the k-smallest value in a given range
=LARGE(range,k)—returns the k-larger value in a given range
=MIN(IF(logical_test,min-range)) (Control-shift-enter)

- logical_test—compares a range of data to an individual criteria
- min_range—the range of data with the values where the needed minimum value is located

=MAX(IF(logical_test,max-range)) (Control-shift-enter)

- logical_test—compares a range of data to an individual criteria
- max_range—the range of data with the values where the needed maximum value is located

Note: Some newer versions of Excel have MINIFS, and MAXIFS functions available. If available the structure is:

=MINIFS(min_range,criteria_range1,criteria1,[criteria_range2, criteria2]...)
=MAXIFS(max_range,criteria_range1,criteria1,[criteria_range2, criteria2]...)

TABLE 6 Extreme Values Example

	A	B	C
1	**New Accounts Opened at New Harbor Bank**		
2	**Customer ID**	**Customer Service Rep**	**Opening Deposit**
3	CID1552	Brian Jones	$3,010
4	CID1636	Cindy Rogers	$221
5	CID1574	Cindy Rogers	$2,913
6	CID1976	Cindy Rogers	$3,870
7	CID1963	Brian Jones	$940
8	CID1803	Brian Jones	N/A
9	CID1619	Cindy Rogers	$4,664
10	CID1837	Cindy Rogers	
11	CID1506	Brian Jones	$4,035
12			
13	**Statistic**	**Opening Deposit**	**Function Structure**
14	Minimum Value	$221	=MIN(C3:C11)
15	Maximum Value	$4,664	=MAX(C3:C11)
16	Smallest Value	$221	=SMALL(C3:C11,1)
17	Largest Value	$4,664	=LARGE(C3:C11,1)
18	Note: These functions ignore blank and non-numeric cells		
19	For the SMALL and LARGE functions, Excel asks for a k value to be input; this value is the first, second, third, and so forth smallest or largest value desired.		
20	**MIN(IF) Example**		
21	**Customer Service Rep**	**Minimum Opening Deposit**	
22	Brian Jones	$940	
23	Cindy Rogers	$0	
24	MIN(IF) Function Structure (from cell B22)		
25	{=MIN(IF($B$3:$B$11=A22,$C$3:$C$11))}		
26	NOTE: This function doesn't ignore blank cells		
27	NOTE: This is an array function and must be entered using **"Control Shift Enter"**		

An example MIN(IF) statement is shown, the MAX(IF) statement structure is the same and therefore not shown.

Video Available: Watch the Chapter 2—Extreme Values Video

Averages

The average is a number expressing the central or typical value in a set of data. There are many averages in statistics, the four most common and the ones we will cover are the mean, the median, the mode, and the weighted mean. Finding the "average" is often one of the first statistics that we compute when we are exploring a variable in a data set. Therefore, it is important to have a firm understanding of what we are finding when we calculate this value. We need to understand what type of average is needed for a given situation as well as whether we are dealing with a population or a sample mean.

- In statistics, we have a **population** if we have a data set that includes all possible members or measurements from a group we are interested in studying. For example, a data set of all female United States citizens would need to include every female in the world that is a citizen of the United States to be considered a population.
- In statistics, we have a **sample** if we have a data set that includes only a subset of all possible members or measurements from a group we are interested in studying. For example, a data set of 1,000 female United States citizens would be a sample because not all females in the world that are a citizen of the United States are included in the data set.

Population and Sample Means

The Mean is the "average" that is most commonly used. To calculate this value, you simply add up the numbers that you want an average of, and then you divide by the total count of the numbers that you want an average of. The average can only be computed for interval-level and ratio-level data. The mathematical formula for the population and sample mean is as follows:

TABLE 7 Population and Sample Mean Formulas

Population Mean $\mu = \frac{\sum_{i=1}^{N} x_i}{N}$	**Sample Mean** $\bar{x} = \frac{\sum_{i=1}^{N} x_i}{n}$

For ungrouped data, the population and sample mean is the sum of all the population or sample values divided by the total number of population or sample values. This is such an important formula, you should be able to calculate the mean with and without using the Excel function which is the AVERAGE function. The Excel AVERAGE function is the same for both populations and samples, the statistic computed depends entirely on the data set.

Where:

- μ represents the population mean. It is the Greek lowercase letter "mu"
- $\bar{x}$ represents the sample mean. It is called "xbar"
- N is the number of values in the population
- n is the number of values in the sample
- X represents any particular value from a population
- x represents any particular value from a sample
- $\sum$ is the Greek capital letter "sigma" and indicates the operation of adding
- $\sum x$ is the mathematical notation indicating to add up the x values in the data

In this text, if you encounter a Greek letter or capital English letter, it will be referring to a population statistics parameter. Sample statistics parameters will be identified using lowercase English letters.

Excel Functions for Finding the Mean

=AVERAGE(range)—Computes the mean of the values in the cells in the given range
=AVERAGEIFS(average_range,criteria_range1,criteria1,[criteria_range2,criteria2]...)

- Computes the mean of the values in the average_range given the criteria is met.
- average_range—Required. The range of cells to find the mean of.
- criteria_range1—Required. The first range in which to evaluate the associated criteria.
- criteria1—Required. The criteria in the form of a number, expression, cell reference, or text that define which cells will be counted. For example, criteria can be expressed as 32, ">32", B4, "apples", or "32".
- criteria_range2, criteria2, ... Optional. Additional ranges and their associated criteria. Up to 127 range/criteria pairs are allowed.

TABLE 8 AVERAGE Functions Example

	A	B	C
1	New Accounts Opened at New Harbor Bank		
2	Customer ID	Customer Service Rep	Opening Deposit
3	CID1552	Brian Jones	$3,010
4	CID1636	Cindy Rogers	$221
5	CID1574	Cindy Rogers	$2,913
6	CID1976	Cindy Rogers	$3,870
7	CID1963	Brian Jones	$940
8	CID1803	Brian Jones	N/A
9	CID1619	Cindy Rogers	$4,664
10	CID1837	Cindy Rogers	
11	CID1506	Brian Jones	$4,035
12			
13	Average Amount of Opening Deposits		$2,808
14	AVERAGE Function Structure (from cell C13)		=AVERAGE(C3:C11)
15			
16	AVERAGEIFS Function Example		
17	Customer Service Rep	Average Amount of Opening Deposits	
18	Brian Jones	$2,662	
19	Cindy Rogers	$2,917	
20	Jim Henderson	#DIV/0!	
21	AVERGAGEIFS Function Structure (from cell B18)		
22	=AVERAGEIFS($C$3:$C$11,$B$3:$B$11,A18)		
23			
24	AVERAGEIFS with IFERROR Function Example		
25	Customer Service Rep	Average Amount of Opening Deposits	
26	Brian Jones	$2,662	
27	Cindy Rogers	$2,917	
28	Jim Henderson		
29	AVERGAGEIFS with IFERROR Function Structure (from cell B26)		
30	=IFERROR(AVERAGEIFS($C$3:$C$11,$B$3:$B$11,A26),"")		

Notice in row 20, the customer service representative Jim Henderson did not have opening deposits in the data set. Therefore the #DIV/0! error in cell C20 is a valid error because the formula requires that we divide the sum of the values by the count of the values and the count is zero in this case. We can remove this error by wrapping the AVERAGEIFS function inside the IFERROR function as shown on row 30.

Video Available: Watch the Chapter 2—The Mean Video

Population and Sample Medians

The Median is the "middle" value in the list of numbers. It is the midpoint of the values after they have been ordered from the lowest to the highest value. The median value is found in exactly the same manner for both populations and samples. The median value may or may not be an actual value in the data set. If the data set contains an even number of observations, then the median value will be the average value between the two values that occupy the middle positions of the ordered data set. If the data set contains an odd number of observations, then the median value will be in the data set and will be the value that occupies the middle position of the ordered data set. The median value is an important value because it is not affected by extremely large or small values as much as the average sometimes is. Also, the median can be found for ordinal-level as well as interval-level and ratio-level data, while the mean can only be computed for interval-level and ratio-level data.

TABLE 10 MEDIAN Values for an Even and Odd Number of Observations

Example data set with an even number of observations	Ages of four college students 19, 20, 21, 22 then the median is the average of 20 and 21 and is 20.5
Example data set with an odd number of observations	Ages of five college students 19, 20, 21, 22, 23 then the median is 21

Excel Functions for Finding the Median

=MEDIAN(range)—returns the median value in a given range
=MEDIAN(IF(logical_test,median-range)) (Control-shift-enter)

- logical_test—compares a range of data to an individual criteria
- median_range—the range of data with the values where the needed median value is located

Note: Some newer versions of Excel have a MEDIANIFS function available. If available the structure is **=MEDIANIFS(median_range,criteria_range1,criteria1,[criteria_range2,criteria2]...)**

TABLE 9 MEDIAN Functions Example

	A	B	C
1	**New Accounts Opened at New Harbor Bank**		
2	**Customer ID**	**Customer Service Rep**	**Opening Deposit**
3	CID1552	Brian Jones	$3,010
4	CID1636	Cindy Rogers	$221
5	CID1574	Cindy Rogers	$2,913
6	CID1976	Cindy Rogers	$3,870
7	CID1963	Brian Jones	$940
8	CID1803	Brian Jones	N/A
9	CID1619	Cindy Rogers	$4,664
10	CID1837	Cindy Rogers	
11	CID1506	Brian Jones	$4,035
12			
13	**Median Amount of Opening Deposits**		$3,010
14	**MEDIAN Function Structure (from cell C13)**		=MEDIAN(C3:C11)
15			
16	**MEDIAN(IF) Function Example**		
17	**Customer Service Rep**	**Median Amount of Opening Deposits**	
18	Brian Jones	$3,010	
19	Cindy Rogers	$2,913	
20	Jim Henderson	#NUM!	
21	MEDIAN(IF) Function Structure (from cell B18)		
22	{=MEDIAN(IF($B$3:$B$11=A18,$C$3:$C$11))}		
23	NOTE: This is an array function and must be entered using **"Control Shift Enter"**		
24	**MEDIANIFS with IFERROR Function Example**		
25	**Customer Service Rep**	**Median Amount of Opening Deposits**	
26	Brian Jones	$3,010	
27	Cindy Rogers	$2,913	
28	Jim Henderson		
29	MEDIAN(IF) with IFERROR Function Structure (from cell B26)		
30	{=IFERROR(MEDIAN(IF($B$3:$B$11=A26,$C$3:$C$11)),"")}		
31	NOTE: This is an array function and must be entered using **"Control Shift Enter"**		

Notice in row 20, the customer service representative Jim Henderson didn't have opening deposits in the data set. Therefore the #NUM! error in cell C20 is a valid error because the function did not find any occurrences of Jim Henderson in the data set. We can remove this error by wrapping the MEDIAN(IF) function inside the IFERROR function as shown on row 30.

Video Available: Watch the Chapter 2—The Median Video

Population and Sample Modes

The Mode is the value that occurs most often in a set of data; therefore, it is the most probable value in the data set. The mode is found in exactly the same manner for both populations and samples. The mode is the only measure of central tendency that can be found for nominal level data; however, it is also valid for ordinal, interval, and ratio level data. A given data set may have zero or more modes depending on the data. In addition, the mode is not affected by extreme outliers.

TABLE 10 MODE Examples

Example data set with zero modes	Ages of five college students 19, 20, 21, 22, 23—since each value occurs only once this data set contains zero modes
Example data set with one mode	Ages of five college students 19, 20, 20, 22, 23—the number 20 occurs the most times, it is the single mode
Example data set with two modes	Ages of five college students 19, 20, 20, 22, 22—the number 20 and 22 both occur the same number of times; therefore, they are both modes

Excel Functions for Finding the Mode

=MODE.SNGL(range)—returns one of the mode values in a given range
=MODE.MULT(range)—returns all the modes in a given range (Control-shift-enter)
=**MODE.SNGL(IF(logical_test,mode-range)) (Control-shift-enter)**

- logical_test—compares a range of data to an individual criteria
- mode_range—the range of data with the values where the needed mode value is located

'ABLE 11 MODE Functions Example

	A	B	C
	ew Accounts Opened at New Harbor Bank		
		Customer Service Rep	Opening Deposit
		Brian Jones	$3,010
		Cindy Rogers	$3,870
		Cindy Rogers	$2,913
		Cindy Rogers	$3,870
		Brian Jones	$3,010
		Brian Jones	N/A
		Cindy Rogers	$4,664
		Cindy Rogers	
		Brian Jones	$4,035
	pening Deposits		$3,010
	ructure (from cell C13)		=MODE.SNGL(C3:C11)
	ening Deposits		
	des of Opening Deposits		
		$3,010	
		$3,870	
	Function Structure (from range B18:B19)		
21	{=MODE.MULT(C3:C11)}		
22	This is an array function and must be entered using **"Control Shift Enter."** Also, this array function must be entered by first selecting the range to be filled in with the modes. This example only had two modes; if unsure about the number of modes in the data set, select a large range for the MODE.MULT fill area to be sure to capture all the modes.		
23	**MODE.SNGL Function Example**		
24	**Customer Service Rep**	**Modes of Opening Deposits**	
25	Brian Jones	$3,010	
26	Cindy Rogers	$3,870	
27	MODE.SNGL Function Structure (from cell B25)		
28	{=MODE.SNGL(IF($B$3:$B$11=A25,$C$3:$C$11))}		
29	This is an array function and must be entered using **"Control Shift Enter."** Also, this array function must be entered by first selecting only one cell and after entering the function, it can then be copied down.		

Video Available: Watch the Chapter 2—The Mode Video

Weighted Mean

The Weighted Mean is the "average" that takes not only the values of a variable into account but also a separate weighting factor. For example, your final grade in a course is most often a weighted average.

TABLE 12 Weighted Mean Formulas

Mathematical Formula	$\bar{x}_w = \frac{\sum_{i=1}^{n} w_i x_i}{\sum_{i=1}^{n} w_i}$
Excel Implementation	$\bar{x}_w = \frac{SUMPRODUCT(w_i x_i)}{SUM(w_i)}$

TABLE 13 Weighted Mean Example

	A	B	C	D	E
1	Weights				
2	HW Weight	Exam Weight	Final Weight		
3	25%	45%	30%		
4					
5	**Student**	**Homework Average**	**Exam Average**	**Final Exam**	**Weighted Average**
6	Student1	91%	87%	77%	84.88%
7	Student2	85%	95%	99%	93.71%
8	Student3	98%	96%	97%	96.91%
9					
10	Weighted Mean Formula Structure (from cell E6)				
11	=SUMPRODUCT(B6:D6,$A$3:$C$3)/SUM($A$3:$C$3)				

Note: If the weights sum to 1, then the dominator is 1 and therefore not required for this special case.

Video Available: Watch the Chapter 2—The Weighted Mean Video

Dispersion (aka Spread)

A measure of location, such as the mean or the median, only describes the center of the data but it does not tell us anything about the spread of the data. For example, if someone told you that the stream ahead averaged 2.5 feet in depth. If you could not swim, would you want to try to cross it without additional information? Probably not. You would want to know something about the variation in the depth. A second reason for studying the dispersion in a set of data is to compare the spread in two or more sets of data.

The first and easiest measure of dispersion is the range in the data. The range is simply the maximum value minus the minimum value. The other two measures of dispersion we will cover are variance and standard deviation.

FIGURE 1 Example Dispersion or Spread in Two Data Sets

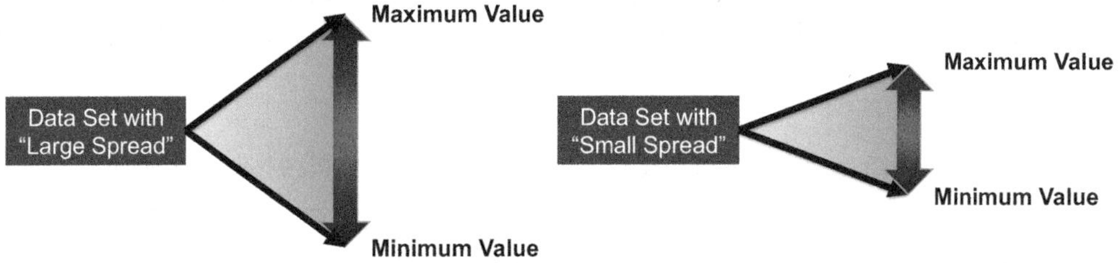

Range = Maximum Value – Minimum Value

TABLE 14 Population and Sample Variance Formulas

Population Variance	Sample Variance
$\sigma^2 = \frac{\sum_{i=1}^{N}(X_i - \mu)^2}{N}$	$s^2 = \frac{\sum_{i=1}^{n}(x_i - \bar{x})^2}{n}$
Excel: = VAR.P(range)	Excel: VAR.S(range)

TABLE 15 Population and Sample Standard Deviation Formulas

Population Standard Deviation	Sample Standard Deviation
$\sigma = \sqrt{\frac{\sum_{i=1}^{N}(X_i - \mu)^2}{N}}$	$s = \sqrt{\frac{\sum_{i=1}^{n}(x_i - \bar{x})^2}{n}}$
Excel: = STDEV.P(range)	Excel: STDEV.S(range)

Where:

- σ^2 represents the population variance. It is the Greek lowercase letter "sigma" squared.
- σ represents the population standard deviation. It is the Greek lowercase letter "sigma."
- s^2 represents the sample variance. s represents the sample standard deviation.
- μ represents the population mean. It is the Greek lowercase letter "mu."
- $\bar{x}$ represents the sample mean. It is called "xbar."
- N is the number of values in the population. n is the number of values in the sample.
- X represents any particular value from a population. X represents any particular value from a sample.
- $\sum$ is the Greek capital letter "sigma" and indicates the operation of adding.

Since, in business the vast majority of the time, we are dealing with samples and not populations, we will show the Excel implementation of the sample variance and standard deviation. However, please note that the implementation of the population variance and standard deviation is the same, the only differences are:

1. The data set needs to include all possible observations from the population.
2. The variance and standard deviation functions for population are VAR.P and STDEV.P instead of VAR.S and STDEV.S.

TABLE 16 Sample Variance and Standard Deviation Example

	A	B	C	D
1	**Employee Number**	**Name**	**Rating**	**Salary**
2	EMP0005043	Lesia Brabham	3	$36,000
3	EMP0002807	Clemente Keane	5	$35,000
4	EMP0004101	Lyndia Earp	5	$37,000
5	EMP0008031	Hope Coley	3	$73,000
6	EMP0001142	Brandie Lollis	4	$84,000
7	EMP0009352	Sheldon Ricco	5	$57,000
8	EMP0006560	Shawanda Gorman	3	$20,000
9	EMP0009207	Ahmad Roper	4	$73,000
10				
11	**Function Name**	**Salary**	**Function Structure**	
12	Range	$64,000.00	=MAX(D2:D9)-MIN(D2:D9)	
13	Variance	532125000	=VAR.S(D2:D9)	
14	Standard Deviation	$23,067.83	=STDEV.S(D2:D9)	
15				
16	**Example STDEV.S (IF) Function**			
17	**Rating**	**Salary Standard Deviation**		
18	3	$27,184.55		
19	4	$7,778.17		
20	5	$12,165.53		
21	STDEV.S (IF) Function Structure (from cell B18)			
22	{=STDEV.S(IF($C$2:$C$9=A18,$D$2:$D$9))}			
23	This is an array function and must be entered using **"Control Shift Enter."**			

Video Available: Watch the Chapter 2—The Dispersion Video

The Empirical Rule

The main advantage of the standard deviation is that it is in the same units as the variable being described and is therefore the most used measure of dispersion. There are many business applications of the standard deviation especially in association with the normal distribution. We will cover some of these applications in upcoming chapters.

For a symmetrical, bell-shaped distribution:

- Approximately 68% of the observations will lie with plus and minus one standard deviation of the mean.
- About 95% of the observations will lie within plus and minus two standard deviations of the mean.
- Practically all (99.7%) will lie within plus and minus three standard deviations of the mean.

FIGURE 2 The Empirical Rule

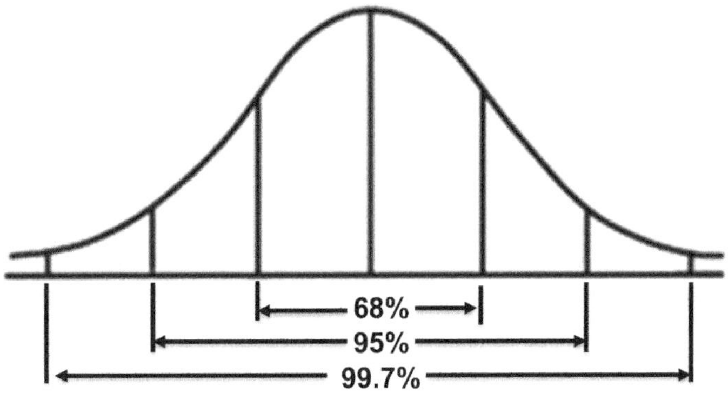

CHAPTER 3

DESCRIPTIVE STATISTICS
Data Visualization

In Chapter 2, we learned how to use some of Excel's conditional descriptive statistics functions like COUNTIFS, SUMIFS, and AVERAGEIFS in order to summarize data. In this chapter, we will learn how to use these functions, as well as others, to create summary tables and charts, which are commonly used in business.

Being able to visualize data correctly is a critical skill that analytic professionals must have in order to understand their own analysis, and to be able to communicate their analysis with others. However, in order to create meaningful visualizations, we often need to create summary tables using rather simple or more complex descriptive functions. In this chapter, we will begin by introducing one of Excel's built-in functionalities called Pivot Tables and Pivot Charts. Pivot Tables allow us to create tables and charts that summarize data in a dynamic manner. However, we cannot always rely on this feature due to certain limitations. However, that is not to say that there are not many benefits of using Pivot Tables to summarize data. In the times where it might not be feasible or convenient to create tables and charts with Excel's Pivot Tables and Charts, we often need to resort to leveraging Excel's built-in functions to create very specific tables and charts that are commonly used in business to summarize data.

Tables and Charts can help answer the following questions:

- How should I organize my summary table?
- What variables should I use for my row and column headings?
- Would adding filters help present my data better?
- How do I compare the relative frequency or percentages of more than one qualitative variable?
- How can I visualize a quantitative variable's distribution?
- How can I compare multiple distributions simultaneously?

Pivot Tables and Pivot Charts

Pivot Tables provide a very efficient way to summarize large amounts of data without the need of manually creating tables based on Excel functions like COUNTIFS, SUMIFS, and AVERAGEIFS. Pivot Tables allow you to control how tables are constructed dynamically by using a "drag and drop" or "click and drag" user interface in an Excel worksheet. The interface allows you to change the organization of your row and column headings quickly. Pivot Charts are created by referencing a Pivot Table. Thus, if you change how a Pivot Table is organized by rows and columns, you will also change the manner in which a Pivot Chart is able to display information. From the combination of Pivot Tables and Pivot Charts, you can explore various ways of presenting data without the need to implement formulas such as COUNTIFS, SUMIFS, and AVERAGEIFS manually. Pivot Tables and Charts are useful because it allows you to find the most useful way of presenting your data.

If you build multiple Pivot Tables and Charts within an Excel Worksheet, you can connect all of the Pivot Tables and Charts by something called a Slicer. Slicers allow you to filter multiple Pivot Tables and Charts within a Workbook. Slicers provide a dynamic way in which you can summarize your data.

Procedure to Create a Pivot Table

1. Select the data you want to include in the Pivot Table.
2. Go to Insert - Pivot Table.
3. Excel will display the "Create PivotTable" dialog with your data selected. In this case, we have selected the "Sales_data" spreadsheet with the range from A1 to K87895.

FIGURE 1 Create PivotTable Dialog Example

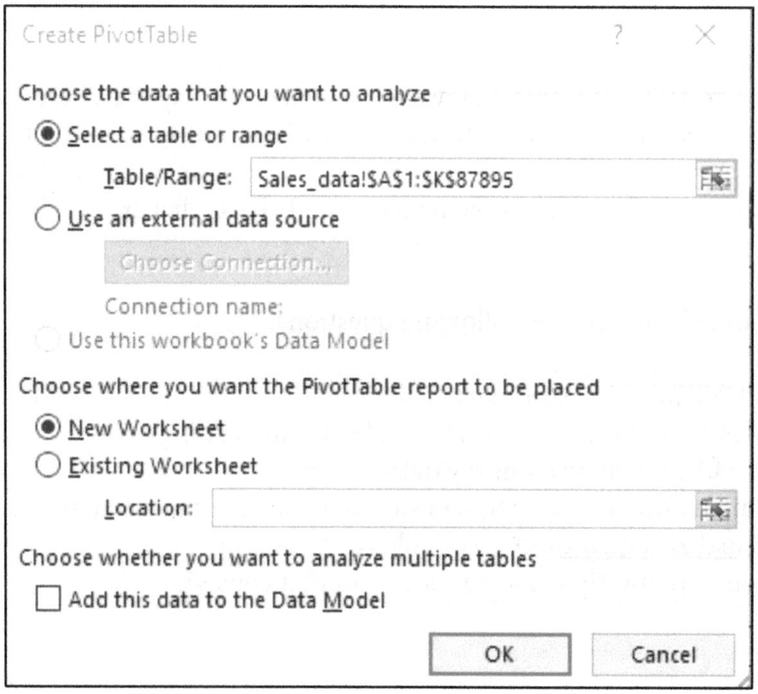

4. In the "Choose where you want the PivotTable report to be placed," select either "New Worksheet" or "Existing Worksheet" and hit OK.
5. Excel will then create a blank PivotTable and open the "PivotTable Fields" dialog. The PivotTable Fields dialog shows all the available columns from the data set you previously selected. From here, you can drag and drop the fields into the various sections of the pivot table.

FIGURE 2 PivotTable Fields Dialog and PivotTable Example

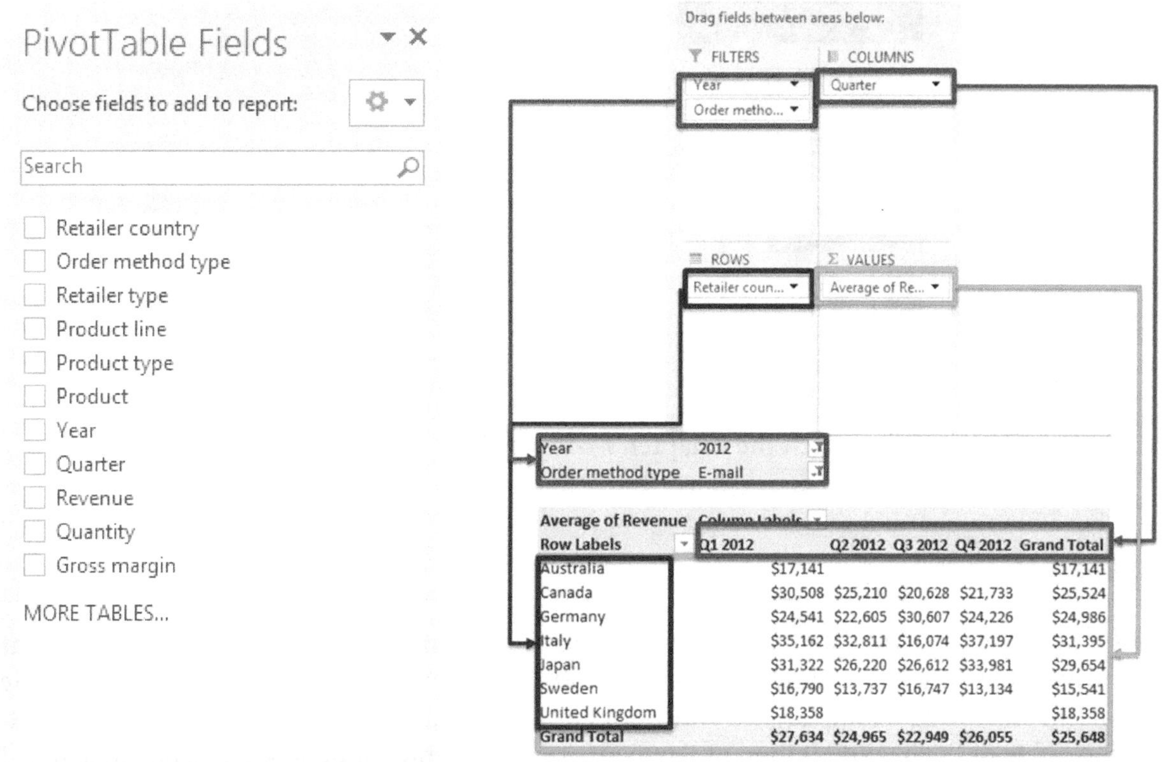

6. In this example, the field "Retailer country" was placed in the rows of the table. The "Quarter" field was placed in the columns of the table. The statistic average of the field "Revenue" was placed in the values area and the fields "Year" and "Order method type" were selected for the filters. To simplify the table and chart, "Quarter" was removed from the columns for Figure 4.

FIGURE 3 Pivot Table Example

Year	(All)
Row Labels	**Total Revenue**
United States	$650,810,961
Japan	$281,665,499
China	$248,823,217
France	$219,523,642
United Kingdom	$219,223,088
Korea	$158,574,133
Belgium	$96,958,570
Grand Total	**$1,875,579,108**

FIGURE 4 Pivot Chart Example

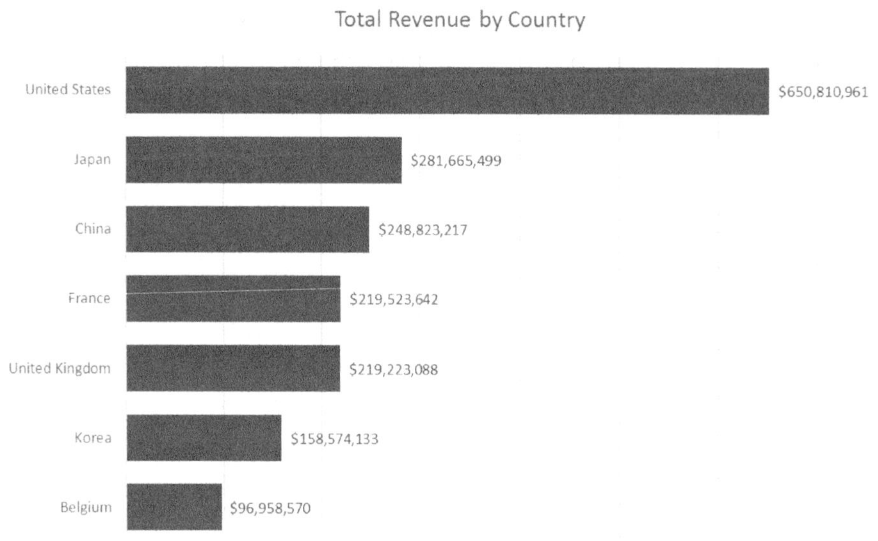

Video Available: Watch the Chapter 3—Pivot Table Video

Qualitative Data

There are two main types of data. The first type is called **qualitative data** and the second type is called **quantitative data**. Simply put, qualitative data is **non-numeric** data and quantitative data is **numeric** data. For the following examples, we will be focusing on qualitative data. For example, Political Affiliation, State of Birth, and Method of Payment are all examples of qualitative data. Since this data is nonnumeric, it can be classified into categories and we can use these categories to summarize data.

As noted, non-numeric data can be grouped into categories, which are often called classes. We can group this type of data into what is called a Frequency Table. Frequency Tables consist of a grouping of qualitative data into mutually exclusive and collectively exhaustive classes. This means that each non-numeric value must fit into at least one class. Furthermore, this non-numeric value can only fit into one class. Frequency Tables allow you to summarize how many times a certain class appears in a particular array of data.

In Table 1, a Frequency and Relative Frequency Table has been created. For this table, there are three distinct categories. These categories include each location (i.e., Marietta, Athens, and Parkersburg) in which vehicles are being sold. The second column of this table shows the Frequency, which in the case represents the number of cars sold at each location. As we noted, Frequency Tables must contain mutually exclusive categories. In this example, the categories (i.e., locations) are mutually exclusive because each vehicle sold is associated with just one location. In addition, Frequency Tables must be collectively exhaustive. For this example, every car that is sold is accounted for in the total count, which makes this Frequency Table valid because it is both mutually exclusive and collectively exhaustive.

When the Frequency is calculated for the mutually exclusive categories, it is also useful to calculate the relative frequency. A Relative Frequency is represented as a percentage because it is a ratio of the individual count divided by the total count from all categories.

TABLE 1 Frequency and Relative Frequency Table Example

	A	B	C
1	**Location**	**Profit per Sale**	**Vehicle-Type**
2	Marietta	$1,387	Sedan
3	Athens	$1,754	SUV
4	Marietta	$1,817	Hybrid
5	Athens	$1,040	Compact
6	Parkersburg	$1,273	Sedan
7	Athens	$1,529	Sedan
8	Parkersburg	$3,082	Truck
9			
10	**Frequency and Relative Frequency Table**		
11	**Location**	**Frequency (Cars Sold)**	**Relative Frequency (% Sold)**
12	Marietta	2	28.6%
13	Athens	3	42.9%
14	Parkersburg	2	28.6%
15	Totals	7	100.0%
16		Formula from cell B12	Formula from cell C12
17		=COUNTIFS($A$2:$A$8,$A12)	=B12/$B$15

A Frequency Table is needed in order to create a Frequency Chart. Frequency Charts are normally created with Bar Charts. These charts simply allow you to compare the similarities or differences between various frequencies (i.e., cars sold by location). Figure 5 shows an example of Frequency Bar Chart.

A bar chart is a graph that shows qualitative classes on the horizontal axis and the class frequencies on the vertical axis. The class frequencies are proportional to the heights of the bars. (Lind, 2015)

FIGURE 5 Frequency Bar Chart Example

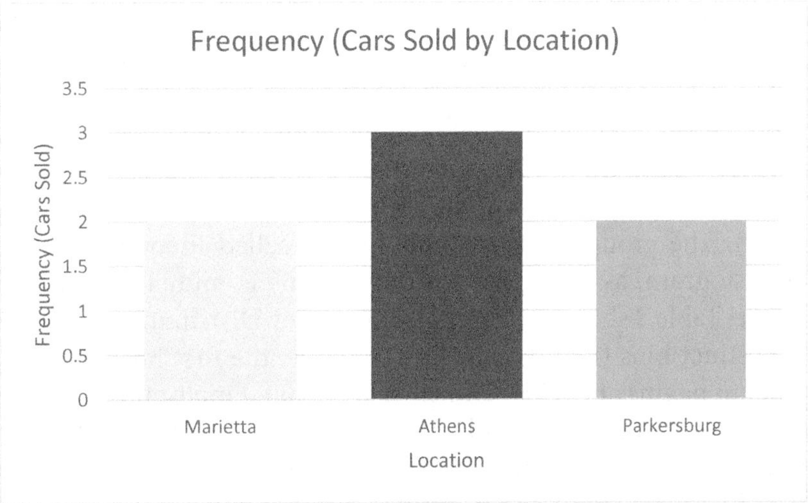

A Relative Frequency Table is needed in order to create a Relative Frequency Chart. Relative Frequency Charts are normally created with Pie Charts. These charts simply allow you to compare the similarities or differences between various percentages (i.e., percent of cars sold by location). Figure 6 shows an example of Relative Frequency Pie Chart.

A pie chart is a graph that shows the proportion or percentage that each class represents the total number of frequencies. (Lind, 2015)

FIGURE 6 Frequency Pie Chart Example

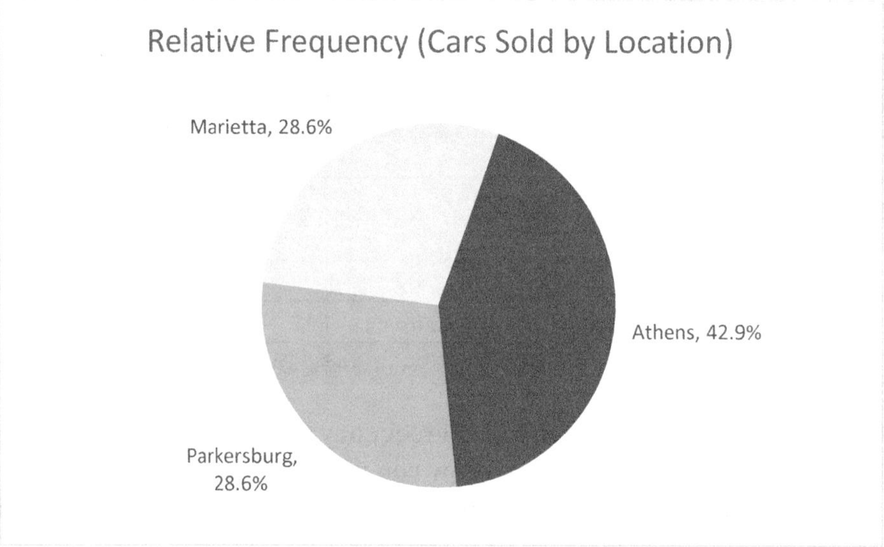

Video Available: Watch the Chapter 3—Qualitative Data

Quantitative Data

In the previous section, we focused on qualitative data and we created Frequency and Relative Frequency Tables and Charts. In this section, we will discuss how to create tables based on **quantitative data.** Remember, quantitative data is **numeric**. For example, cost, revenue, profit, age, and salary are all forms of quantitative data.

It may not be intuitive, but quantitative data can be grouped into classes and these classes can be used to create Frequency Distributions. If a quantitative variable is used to create classes, we often call these classes "bins." A bin begins at some sort of numeric value (i.e., $1,000) and ends at another numeric value ($1,700). The grouping of multiple bins is called Frequency Distribution, or more commonly called a Histogram, as long as the group of bins is mutually exclusive and collectively exhaustive. For example, Table 2 shows an Example Frequency Distribution, where Profit per Sale was used to create three distinct bins (i.e., classes). For example, the first bin begins at $1,000 and ends at $1,700. The second bin begins at $1,700, and ends at $2,500. Finally, the third bin begins at $2,500 and ends at $3,200. For this example, we would like to know how many vehicles that were sold would fit into each profit class. Since each vehicle can only be sold in one profit class, we would say that the bins would satisfy the requirement of being mutually exclusive. Likewise, our bins allow us to be collectively exhausted because each Profit per Sale can fit into one of the three bins.

It should be noted that the lowest bin should start at a value that is less than or equal to the minimum value that is being summarized. Likewise, the highest bin should end at a value that is greater than or equal to the maximum value that is being summarized.

We can calculate the frequency for each bin by using a simple COUNTIFS. However, you will notice that we need to be careful when considering using equalities or inequalities within the formulas that we develop. We need to be careful because we need to maintain the requirement that the table and the associated bins must be mutually exclusive and collectively exhausted. In other words, no matter what the value of profit is, we need to ensure that it is counted once and only once. Thus, you will notice that the formula in B12 is developed with a combination of inequalities (i.e., ">=" and "<") so we make sure that any value of profit is counted once and only once. For example, if Profit per Sale were exactly equal to $1,700, it would be included in the second bin.

Once we have the Frequency Distribution (i.e., Histogram), it is useful to calculate the "cumulative percentage," which is the number of observations in a bin, divided by the total frequency plus the previous cumulative percentage value. This value captures the percentage of the total for each class. Quantitative data can also be summarized graphically via histograms and frequency Polygons.

TABLE 2 Frequency Distribution Example

	A	B	C
1	**Location**	**Profit per Sale**	**Vehicle-Type**
2	Marietta	$1,387	Sedan
3	Athens	$1,754	SUV
4	Marietta	$1,817	Hybrid
5	Athens	$1,040	Compact
6	Parkersburg	$1,273	Sedan
7	Athens	$1,529	Sedan
8	Parkersburg	$3,082	Truck
9			
10		**Frequency Distribution of Profits**	
11	**Profit Class**	**Frequency**	**Cumulative %**
12	$1,000 up to $1,700	4	57.1%
13	$1,700 up to $2,500	2	85.7%
14	$2,500 up to $3,200	1	100.0%
15	Totals	7	100.0%
16		Formula from cell B12	Formulas from cell C12 and C13
17		=COUNTIFS($B$2:$B$8,">= 1000", $B$2:$B$8,"<1700")	=B12/$B$15 =C12+B13/$B$15
18			

19	Number of Observations (n)	7	=COUNT(B2:B8)
20	Try k=1	2	=2^1
21	Try k=2	4	=2^2
22	Try k=3, satisfies $2^k > n$	8	=2^3
23			
24	Maximum Value	$3,082	=MAX(B2:B8)
25	Minimum Value	$1,040	=MIN(B2:B8)
26	Class Interval Needed	700	=ROUND((B24-B25)/3,-2)

The Histogram shown in Figure 7 can be created by using the data found in Table 2.

A Histogram is a graph in which the classes are marked on the horizontal axis and the class frequencies on the vertical axis. The class frequencies are represented by the heights of the bars, and the bars are drawn adjacent to each other. (Lind, 2015)

FIGURE 7 Histogram Example

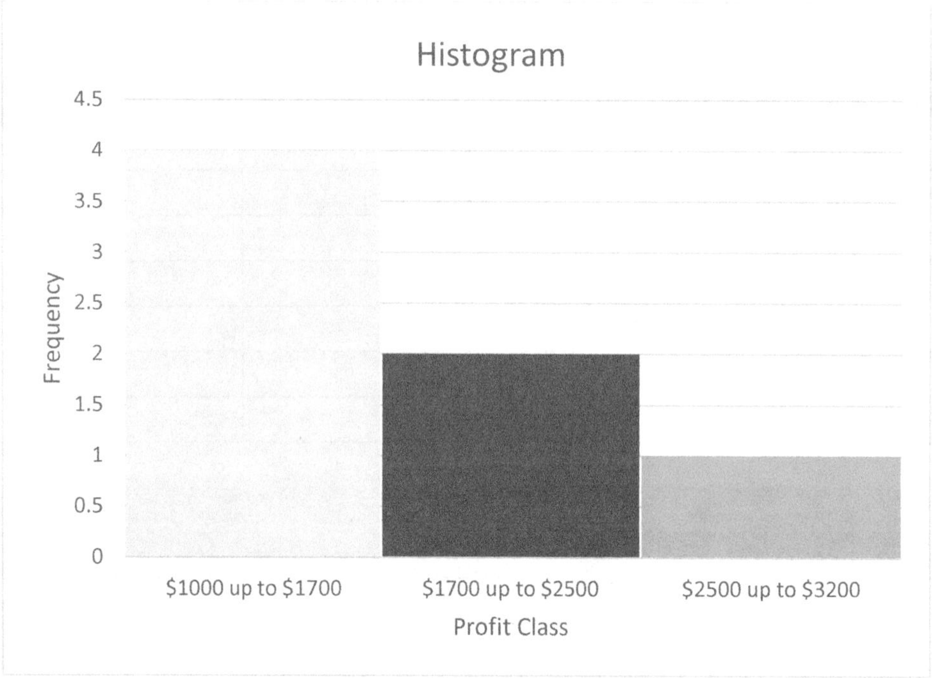

A Frequency Polygon is similar to a histogram; it also shows the shape of a distribution. It consists of line segments connecting the class midpoints of the class frequencies. (Lind, 2015)

A Frequency Polygon is an alternative way to view a Histogram. An example of a Frequency Polygon is shown in Figure 8. Rather than using a Bar Chart for a Histogram, a Frequency Polygon simply uses a Line Chart. A Frequency Polygon is very useful when you are trying to compare multiple Histograms on the same chart.

FIGURE 8 Frequency Polygon Example

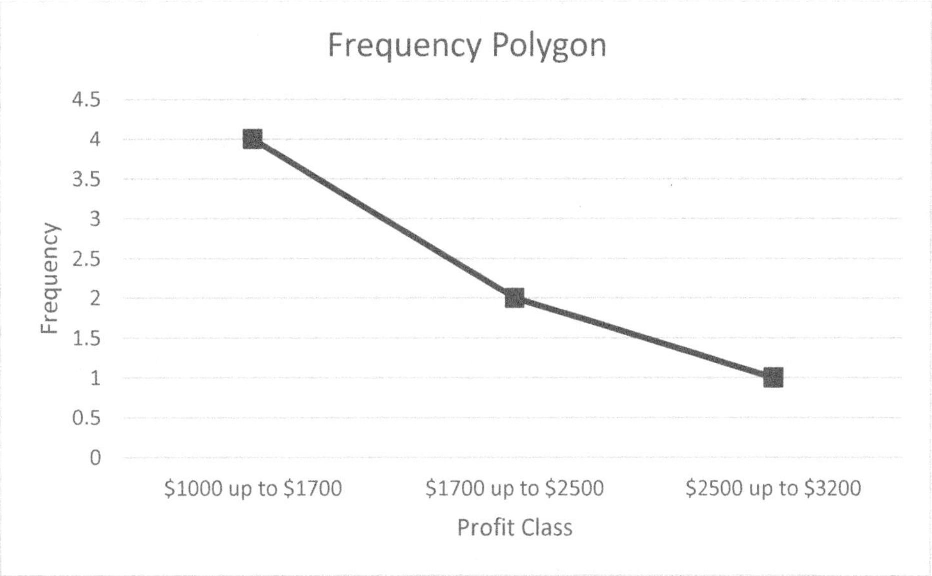

Steps to Creating a Frequency Distribution

Histograms and Frequency Polygons are very useful in order to summarize a quantitative variable's distribution. As noted, when creating bins, it is important that we can guarantee that the Frequency Distribution is mutually exclusive and collectively exhausted. However, there is no set rule to determine the number of bins that are required nor the bin's starting and ending values. However, there are accepted practices that can be followed. For example, consider the following steps in order to determine the number of bins and each bin's interval.

1. **Determining the number of bins:** A useful method to determine the number of classes is the "**2 to the k rule,**" such that $\mathbf{2^k > n}$, where k is the number of classes and n is the number of observations for a given variable. For example, consider that Table 3 is referencing the data found in Table 2. From the previous example, n is equal to 7 because 7 vehicles were sold. Since n is given, we need to find k such that 2^k is greater than n. It should be noted that k should be the smallest number that satisfies the $2^k > n$ equation. In other words, it not wise to pick a large number for k just to satisfy the equation. K should be found by trial and error starting with low values for K. For example, we can start our search at 1, and try 2, and then try 3. At a value of 3, 2 to the power of 3 (i.e., 2^3) would equal 8, which is greater than 7. Thus, k equaling 3 is the minimum number that satisfies the $2^k > n$ relationship.

TABLE 3 Determining the Number of Bins Example

19	Number of Observations (n)	7	=COUNT(B2:B8)
20	Try k=1	2	=2^1
21	Try k=2	4	=2^2
22	Try k=3, satisfies $2^k > n$	8	=2^3
23	Therefore, the number of classes or bins (k) is 3		

2. **Determining the bin's interval:** Now we must use the relationship of **i >= (H-L)/k** to find the interval width of each bin. For this relationship, i is the class interval that we are trying to find, H is the maximum observed value, L is the minimum observed value, and k is the number of classes. Since H, L, and k are known, we simply need to calculate the right-hand side of the inequality. This calculation would result in a value of 680.667. In this case, it is common to round this number up to a nice "round" number. However, it is not necessary. We could simply round this value up using ROUNDUP to 681, or perhaps we can want a value rounded to the nearest hundredths place. If this is the case, we can use the ROUND function and indicate that the "num_digits" is -2.

TABLE 4 Calculation for Class Intervals Needed Example

24	Maximum Value	$3,082	=MAX(B2:B8)
25	Minimum Value	$1,040	=MIN(B2:B8)
26	Min Class Interval Needed	$681	=(B24-B25)/3
27	Rounded Class Interval Needed	$700	=ROUNDUP(B26,-2)

3. **Set the individual class limits:** Using the rounded class interval and the minimum and maximum set convenient class limits that cover the entire range of data. A guideline is to make the lower limit of the first class a multiple of the class interval.

TABLE 5 Individual Class Limits Example

Profit Class
$1,000 up to $1,700
$1,700 up to $2,500
$2,500 up to $3,200
Totals

4. **Build the Frequency Distribution Table:** A COUNTIFS function can be used to compute each frequency. For consistency, the lower limit is included in the class; however, the upper limit is not included. Therefore, the lower limit includes the equal sign ">=" and the upper limit does not include the equal sign "<". The final Frequency Distribution is shown in Table 6.

TABLE 6 Frequency Distribution Example

Frequency Distribution of Profits		
Profit Class	**Frequency**	**Cumulative %**
$1,000 up to $1,700	4	57.1%
$1,700 up to $2,500	2	85.7%
$2,500 up to $3,200	1	100.0%
Totals	7	100.0%

Video Available: Watch the Chapter 3—Quantitative Data

Bivariate Data

Up to this point, we have dealt mostly with univariate data. In other words, we have been summarizing a single variable. When we have summarized univariate data, we have summarized these values by creating various tables and charts such as frequency tables, bar charts, pie charts, frequency distributions, and frequency polygons. In this section, we will investigate summarizing bivariate data, which means that we will be investigating the relationship between two variables.

Contingency Tables are useful in summarizing the counts or frequencies between two qualitative variables. In other words, the row headings might be one qualitative variable, while the column headings might be another qualitative variable. Contingency Tables are very useful if you need detailed information about the counts between the two qualitative variables being summarized. However, it is difficult to create meaningful visualizations of these tables and therefore it is not common practice to graph them.

For an example of a Contingency Table, consider Table 7. The Contingency Table shown here is a count of how many of each vehicle type was sold at each dealership location. It provides a picture of the interrelationship between two non-numeric or qualitative variables; in this case, location and vehicle type.

A contingency table is a two-variable table that is useful for examining relationships between qualitative variables. Entries can be frequency counts or relative frequencies. (Lind, 2015)

TABLE 7 Contingency Table Example

	A	B	C	D
1	**Location**	**Profit per Sale**	**Vehicle-Type**	**Age of Buyer**
2	Marietta	$1,387	Sedan	28
3	Athens	$1,754	Truck	40
4	Marietta	$1,817	Truck	48
5	Athens	$2,140	Truck	24
6	Parkersburg	$1,273	Sedan	20
7	Athens	$1,529	Sedan	32
8	Parkersburg	$3,082	Truck	56
9				
10	**Contingency Table**			
11	**Location**	**Sedan**	**Truck**	**Total**
12	Marietta	1	1	2
13	Athens	1	2	3
14	Parkersburg	1	1	2
15	Total	3	4	7
16		Formula from cell B12		Formula from cell D12
17		=COUNTIFS($A$2:$A$8,$A12,$C$2:$C$8,B$11)		=SUM(B12:C12)

Scatter Plots, or XY Scatter Plots, show the relationship between two quantitative variables. Based on Scatter Plots we can visually see how one variable is correlated to another variable. In addition, we can visualize if there are certain trends in these relationships. Scatter Plots are created where one quantitative variable is plotted on the chart's X-axis, while the other quantitative variable is plotted on the chart's Y-axis. Individual points on a Scatter Plot are not connected by lines. The relationship between the X and Y variables is visualized as a collection of individual data points on a graph.

For an example of a Scatter Plot, consider Figure 9. The scatter plot shows the relationship between the age of buyer and the profit per sale. It shows a moderate positive relationship between the two variables.

SCATTER PLOT: A two-variable chart that is useful for examining relationships between quantitative variables. One variable is scaled along the X-axis and the other along the Y-axis. (Lind, 2015)

FIGURE 9 Scatter Plot Example

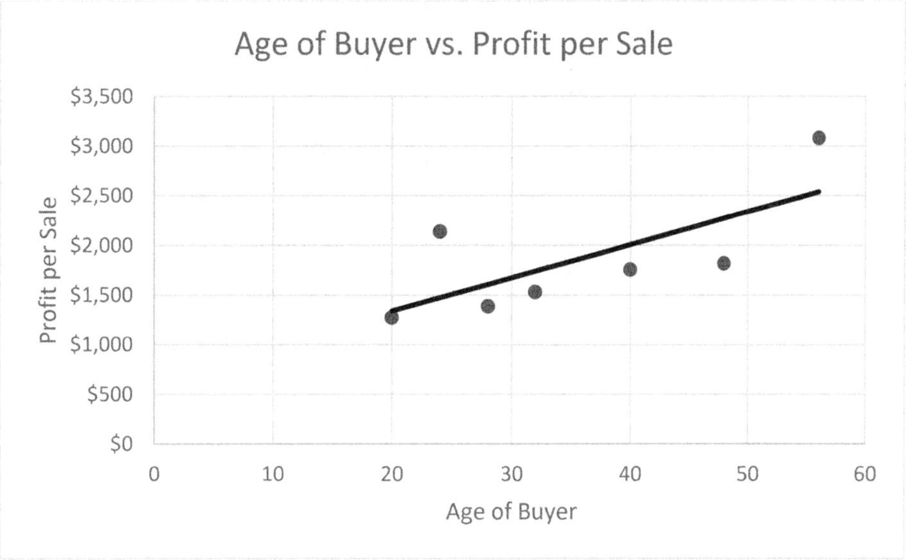

Previously, we noted that correlation in Figure 9 was a moderate and positive relationship between the Age of Buyer and the Profit per Sale. So how was that determined? Consider the following definitions:

The **correlation coefficient (r)** describes the strength of the relationship between two sets of variables. It is calculated using the **CORREL function** in Excel.

- It ranges from -1 up to +1
- A value near 0 indicates there is little linear relationship between the variables
- A value near 1 indicates a positive linear relationship between the variables
- A value near -1 indicates a negative linear relationship between the variables

FIGURE 10 Correlation Scale

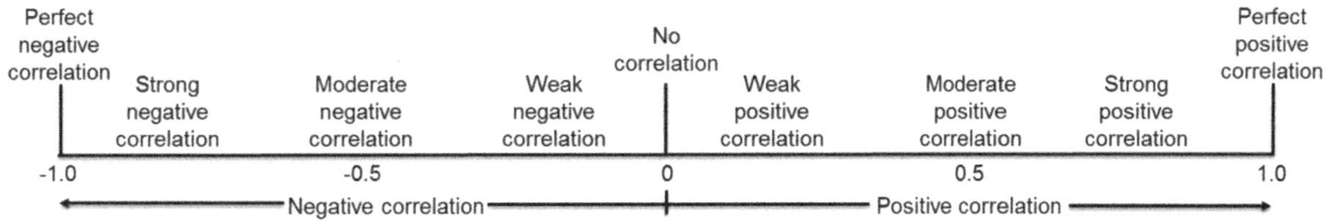

Consider the following examples shown in Table 8. In this example, we are visualizing the relationship between the age of a truck and the cost of maintenance. Using the guidelines for correlation and the coefficient of determination, we could conclude that the correlation is strong and positive. In addition, since the value of the coefficient of determination is rather high, we can say that the age of the truck is a good indicator of predicting the maintenance cost.

TABLE 8 Scatter Plot With Strong Positive Correlation Example

	A	B
1	**Age of Truck**	**Maint. Cost**
2	1	$1,500
3	2	$3,500
4	2	$3,000
5	2	$4,000
6	3	$6,377
7	3	$5,305
8	3	$5,797
9	3	$4,367
10	4	$7,985
11	4	$6,407
12	4	$6,297
13	4	$8,717
14	5	$10,590
15	5	$9,284
16	5	$10,135
17	5	$11,552
18	5	$11,999
19	**Correlation**	95%
20	=CORREL(A2:A18,B2:B18)	

FIGURE 11 Scatter Plot With Strong Positive Correlation Example

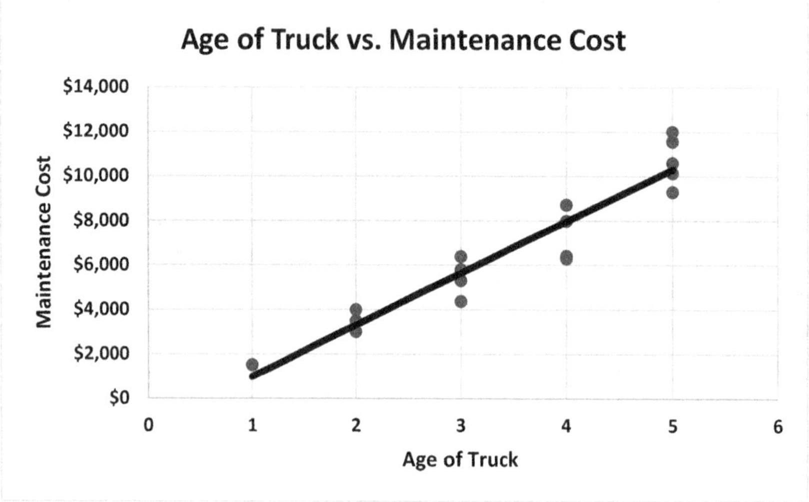

Consider the following examples shown in Table 9. In this example, we are visualizing the relationship between a vehicle's odometer reading and the price the vehicle was sold at an auction. Using the guidelines for correlation and the coefficient of determination, we could conclude that the correlation is strong and negative.

TABLE 9 Scatter Plot With Strong Negative Correlation Example

	A	B
24	Odometer	Auction Price
25	25579	$20,196
26	29273	$21,537
27	12494	$24,037
28	25870	$19,920
29	17262	$22,095
30	41382	$18,854
31	35412	$18,466
32	49199	$17,153
33	32212	$16,477
34	48130	$13,415
35	66537	$12,882
36	58309	$10,396
37	61886	$11,873
38	66926	$14,946
39	67937	$12,340
40	87295	$7,264
41	79685	$8,569
42	79664	$9,604
43	87832	$9,465
44	**Correlation**	-95%
45	=CORREL(A25:A43,B25:B43)	

FIGURE 12 Scatter Plot With Strong Negative Correlation Example

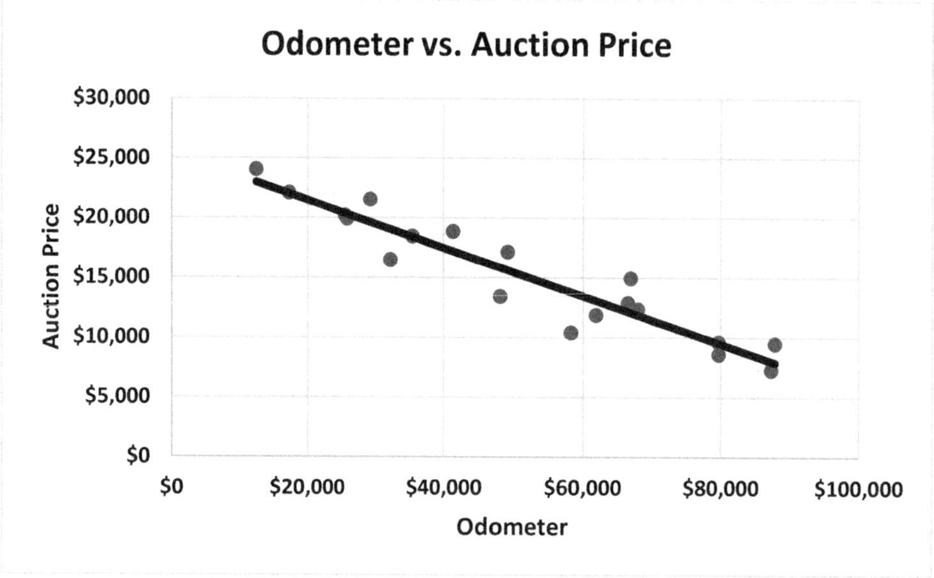

Video Available: Watch the Chapter 3—Bivariate Data

Box and Whisker Plots

Box and whisker plots are very popular amongst statisticians and data analysts. Box and Whisker Plots can help determine if a quantitative variable's distribution is symmetrical or skewed, or whether the outliers are present in the variable.

A box and whisker plot is a graphical display based on quartiles that helps us picture a set of data. They can be helpful in revealing skewness and outliers in a distribution. (Lind, 2015)

The parts of a box and whisker plot include:

- Outliers are extreme, either negative or positive, data points that diverge greatly from the overall pattern of data. As a "rule of thumb," an extreme value is considered an outlier if it is at least 1.5 interquartile ranges below the 1st Quartile or above the 3rd Quartile.
- The line at the top of the whisker is the maximum value excluding outliers.
- The length of the whisker indicates the distance between the 3rd Quartile value and the maximum value.

- The Box contains all values from the 1st Quartile value to the 3rd Quartile. The bottom and top of the box reflects the 1st and 3rd Quartile values.
- The line at the bottom of the whisker is the minimum value excluding outliers.

FIGURE 13 Box and Whisker Plot Diagram

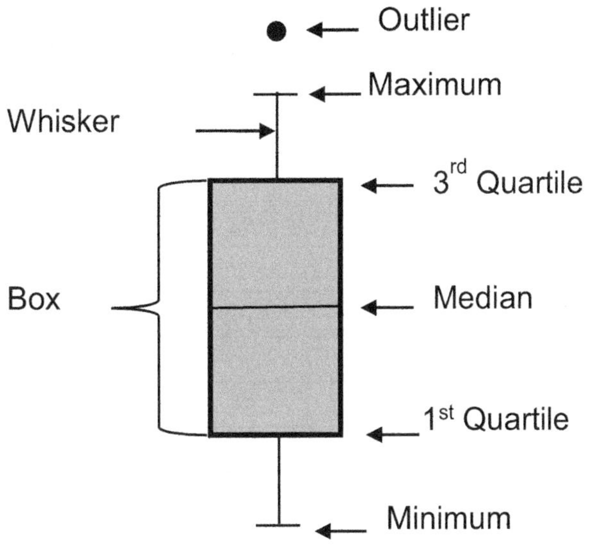

A box and whisker plot can be implemented in Excel by selecting "Insert," Statistical charts, Box and Whisker from the ribbon. Also, the box and whisker plot statistics can be calculated using the **QUARTILE.INC function**. This function requires inputs of the data range and the statistical parameter desired, the parameters available are:

- 0 for the minimum value
- 1 for the 1st quartile (25th percentile) value
- 2 for the median value (50th percentile) value
- 3 for the 3rd quartile (75th percentile) value
- 4 for the maximum value

Outliers can be found by first finding the upper and lower outlier boundaries, and then identifying any values outside of these boundaries. See Table 10 for the Excel calculations needed to identify outliers.

TABLE 10 Box and Whisker Spreadsheet Example

	A	B	C
1	**Regional Sales**		
2	**Month**	**West**	
3	January	70	
4	February	50	
5	March	37	
6	April	36	
7	May	39	
8	June	54	
9	July	9	
10	August	19	
11	September	30	
12	October	25	
13	November	27	
14	December	7	
15			
16		**Regional Sales**	
17	**Statistic**	**Parameter**	**West**
18	Minimum	0	7.0
19	1st Quartile	1	23.5
20	Median	2	33.0
21	3rd Quartile	3	41.8
22	Maximum	4	70.0
23	Mean	N/A	33.6
24	Range	N/A	63.0
25		Formula with C18	
26		=QUARTILE.INC($B$3:$B$14,B18)	
27			
28		**Outlier Calculation**	
29		Difference between Q3 and Q1	
30		Intra-quartile range = IQR	
31	IQR	18.3	=C21-C19
32	IQR*1.5	27.4	=B31*1.5
33	Upper Outlier Boundary:	69.1	=C21+B32
34	Lower Outlier Boundary:	-3.9	=C19-B32

FIGURE 14 Box and Whisker Plot Example

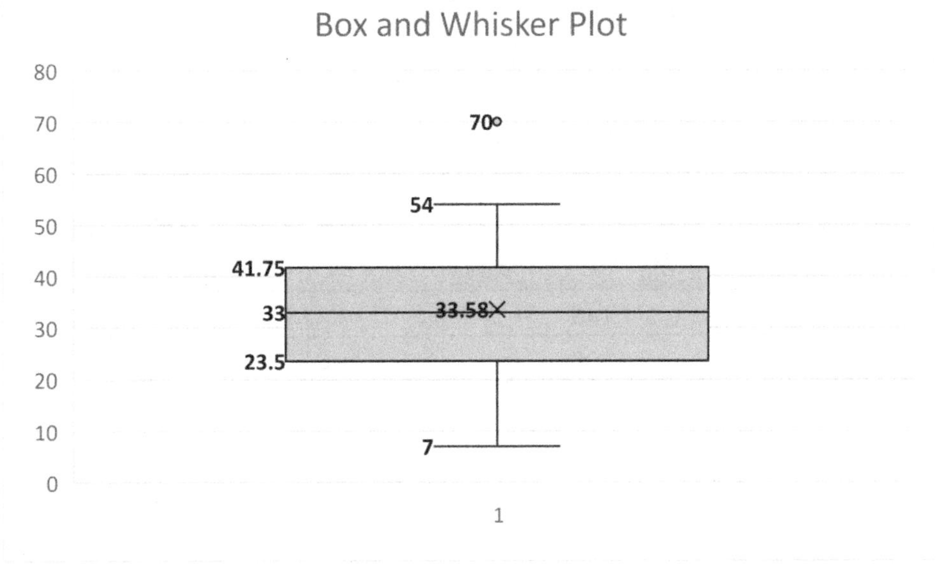

Video Available: Watch the Chapter 3—Box_Plots

Pareto Charts

Pareto Charts are named after Vilfredo Pareto, who was an Italian economist during the late 1800s and early 1900s. Vilfredo is known for the Pareto Principle, which is often referred to as the 80/20 rule (i.e., the law of the vital few). An example of this rule might be 80% of the country's wealth is owned by 20% of the country's population. Another example might include 80% of a company's product might be purchased by 20% of the company's customers.

Pareto analysis is a technique for tallying the number and type of defects that happen within a product or service. (Lind, 2015)

Pareto Charts can be used to summarize a wide variety of problems in business. The X-axis of a Pareto Chart is a list of categories from a qualitative variable (i.e., customers). One special feature of a Pareto Chart is that the numeric frequencies of these categories are sorted in descending order (largest to smallest). Like other charts, Pareto Charts graph the frequency of occurrence of some quantitative variable. However, unlike most charts, Pareto Charts usually consist of two Y-axis. The first, or primary, Y-axis normally represents the numeric count or frequency (i.e., the count of products sold), while the second, or secondary, Y-axis represents the cumulative percent of the frequencies (i.e., percent of products sold).

For an example of a Pareto Chart, consult Table 11 and consider the following business scenario.

The city manager of Athens, Ohio, is concerned with water usage, particularly in single-family homes. The manager would like to develop a plan to reduce the water usage in Athens. To investigate, the manager selects a sample of 100 homes and determines the typical daily water usage for various purposes. The sample results are shown in Table 11.

TABLE 11 Pareto Chart Spreadsheet Example

	A	B	C	D
1	**Reason for Water Usage**	**Gallons per Day**	**Percent of Use**	**Cumulative Percent of Use**
2	Watering	145	42.0%	42.0%
3	Bathing	108	31.3%	73.3%
4	Pool	29	8.4%	81.7%
5	Laundering	25	7.2%	89.0%
6	Dishwashing	13	3.8%	92.8%
7	Car Washing	11	3.2%	95.9%
8	Drinking	8	2.3%	98.3%
9	Cooking	6	1.7%	100.0%
10	Total	345	100.0%	100.0%
11			Formula from C2	Formula from D3
12			=B2/$B$10	=D2+C3

To create the Pareto Chart as shown in Figure 15, follow the steps below.

1. Ensure the data is sorted in descending order (i.e., largest to smallest). In this case, are sorting the Gallons per Day.
2. Calculate the percentages based on the reason water is being used in the city.
3. Calculate the cumulative percentages based on the reason water is being used in the city.
4. Create a Bar chart where the X-axis represents the categories of water usage. Then, ensure that Gallons per Day is the primary Y-axis. Finally, make sure that cumulative percent is the secondary Y-axis.
5. Finally, format as you see fit.

FIGURE 15 Pareto Chart Example

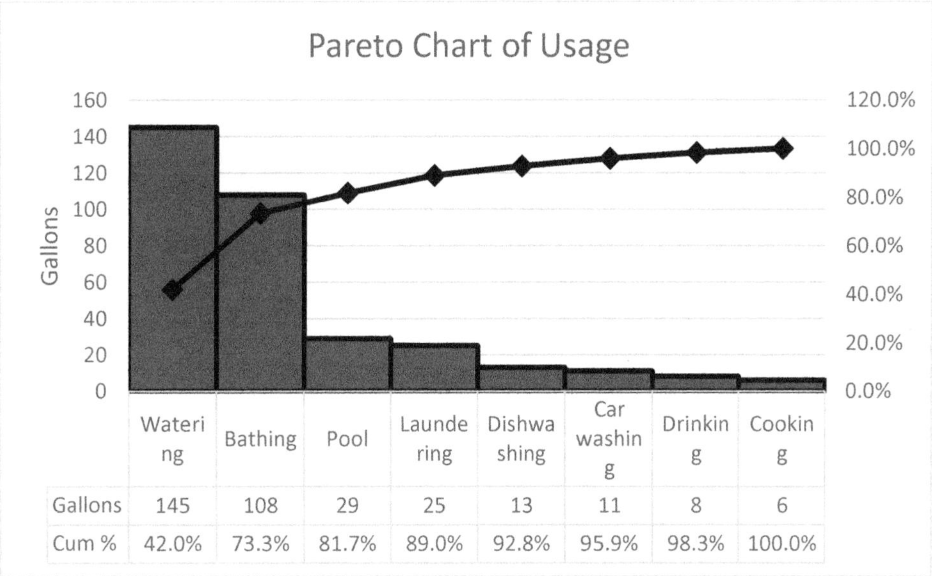

Reference

Lind, D. A. (2015). *Statistical Techniques in Business & Economics Six*. New York, NY: McGraw-Hill Education.

CHAPTER 4

INFERENTIAL STATISTICS
Probability

Up to this point, we have studied descriptive statistics and have learned how to summarize data using tables and charts. We now turn to the second major part of descriptive analytics, namely inferential statistics. Inferential statistics is the science of computing the chance that something will occur in the future based on data collected from the past or present. Inferential statistics techniques also allow us to use sample information in order to make generalizations about the population from which the samples were drawn. As business leaders, we seldom have complete information needed in order to make decisions. The root word of "Inferential" is "Infer" which means to make deductions or conclusions based on known facts. Since most of the time we do not have complete information, we need to use statistical concepts to help us make the best decisions for our business enterprise. The better we understand these concepts, the better we can apply them in the workplace, and the better our business decisions will be.

Basic Definitions

- Inferential Statistics: Computing the chance that something will occur in the future. Gives us the ability to make conclusions about a population based on a sample taken from that population.
- Probability is a value between zero and one, inclusive, describing the relative possibility (chance or likelihood) an event will occur.
- An experiment is a process that leads to the occurrence of one and only one of several possible observations. Each possible outcome can be specified in advance. The outcome of the experiment depends on chance.
- An outcome is the particular result of an experiment.
- An event is the collection of one or more outcomes of an experiment.
  - Events are mutually exclusive if the occurrence of any one event means that none of the others can occur at the same time.
  - Events are independent if the occurrence of one event does not affect the occurrence of another.
  - Events are collectively exhaustive if at least one of the events must occur when an experiment is conducted.

Assigning Probability for One Event Experiments

- **Classical Probability** is based on the assumption that the outcomes of an experiment are equally likely. Example: an experiment of rolling a six-sided die. (Lind, 2015)

$$\text{Classical Probability} = \frac{\text{Number of favorable outcomes}}{\text{Total number of possible outcomes}}$$

- **Empirical Probability** is the probability of an event happening and is the fraction of the time similar events happened in the past. Based on Law of Large Numbers (i.e., over a large number of trials, the empirical probability of an event will approach its true probability). Example: one coin toss, empirical probability is zero or one, as number of coin tosses increases, the empirical probability approaches 0.5. (Lind, 2015)

$$\text{Empirical Probability} = \frac{\text{Number of times the event occurs}}{\text{Total number of observations}}$$

- **Subjective Probability** is the likelihood (probability) of a particular event happening that is assigned by an individual based on whatever information is available. There is little or no past experience or information to base probability. (Lind, 2015) Example: Estimating the likelihood the Cleveland Browns will play in the Super Bowl next year, it is based on the available information.

FIGURE 1 Probability Rule Decision Tree

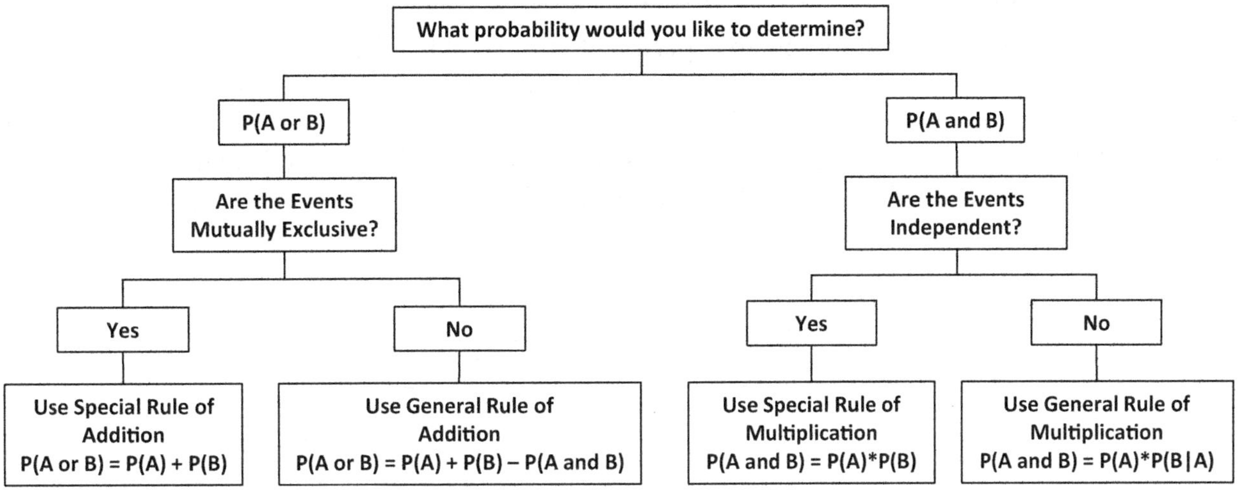

Assigning Probability for Two or More Event Experiments

- Events are mutually exclusive if the occurrence of any one event means that none of the others can occur at the same time. Example: The variable "gender" presents mutually exclusive outcomes, male and female. An employee selected at random is either male or female but cannot be both.
- Events are independent if the occurrence of one event does not affect the occurrence of another. One way to think about independence is to assume that events A and B occur at different times. For example, when event B occurs after event A occurs, does A have any effect on the likelihood that event B occurs? If the answer is no, then the events are independent.
- P(A or B) is the probability of event A or event B occurring.
- P(A and B) is the probability of event A and event B occurring, which is also call joint probability and it is the likelihood that two or more events will happen concurrently.
- P(A|B) is the probability of event B occurring given that the event A has already occurred, probability B given A, which is also called conditional probability.
- The complement rule is used to determine the probability of an event occurring by subtracting the probability of the event not occurring from 1 (i.e., P(A)+P(~A)=1 or P(A) = 1 – P(~A))

Principles of Counting

If the number of possible outcomes in an experiment is small, it is relatively easy to count them. For example, when rolling a die, there are six possible outcomes: 1 pip, 2 pips, 3 pips, 4 pips, 5 pips, and 6 pips. If, however, there are a large number of possible outcomes, such as the number of pips for an experiment with 10 tosses, it would be tedious to count all the possibilities. To help us with counting, we have three formulas available in the decision tree as follows:

FIGURE 2 Principles of Counting Decision Tree

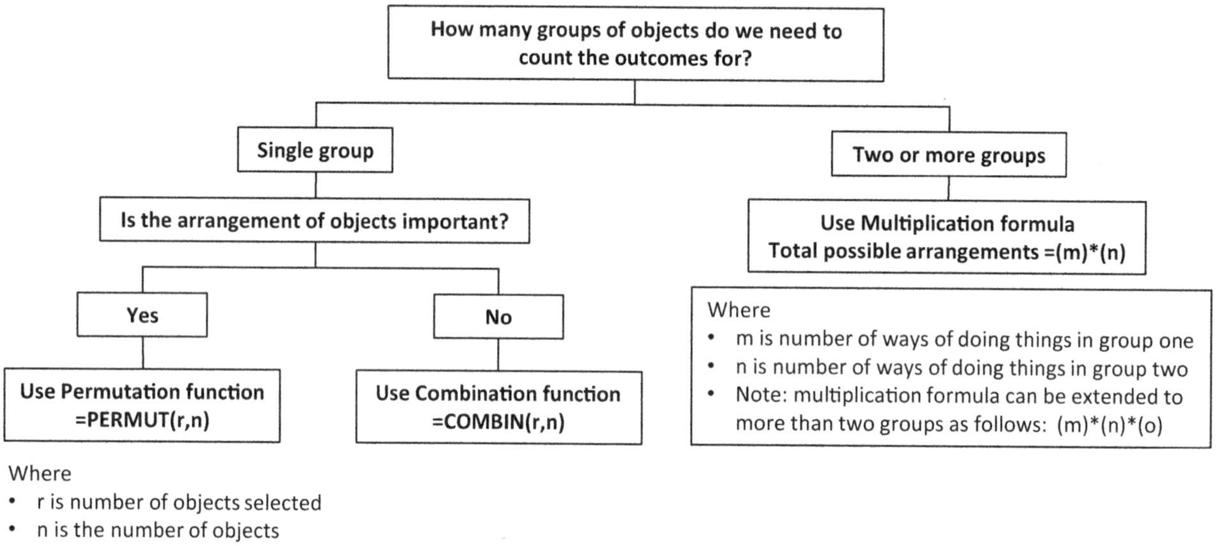

A good example using permutation and combination would be a lottery, depending on the rules associated with the lottery. If the lottery is set up such that the arrangement of the winning numbers is important, such as 1, 5, 10, 15, 20, 34 then we would use the Excel PERMUT function to calculate the possible outcomes. If the lottery is set up such that the arrangement of the winning numbers is not important, such as 5, 1, 34, 10, 20, 15, then we would use the Excel COMBIN function to calculate the possible outcomes. Table 1 shows the number of possible outcomes and chance of winning the classic Ohio Lottery which allows people to select 6 integers from 1 to 49. The arrangement of the numbers drawn is not important so the numbers can be drawn in any order to match tickets with numbers ordered in ascending order. Both the PERMUT and COMBIN functions are shown to stress the importance that arrangement has to increase the total number of possible outcomes and hence the large decrease in the chance of winning. Luckily, winning the lottery does not depend on the arrangement of the numbers drawn so we have much better odds of winning. Therefore, a person buying one ticket for the Classic Ohio Lottery has a 1 in about 14 million chance of winning, which while much better than the 1 in 10 billion chance if arrangement were to be important, is still not good odds. A person could win the lottery every time by purchasing all possible combinations of numbers but they would need to spend almost $14 million in order to guarantee winning, given that each ticket costs $1. If the jackpot was over $14 million then they could possibly profit if they were to be the only winner. However, in addition to the risk of multiple winners reducing the payoff, another disadvantage would be they would be trading after-tax dollars for before-tax dollars so this would also greatly reduce or eliminate any chance of profit.

TABLE 1 Calculation of Possible Outcomes Using PERMUT and COMBIN Example

	A	B
1	**Chance of Winning Lottery Calculator**	
2	Numbers to pick from	49
3	Numbers selected	6
4		
5	**Arrangement Important**	
6	**Possible Outcomes**	**Formula**
7	10,068,347,520	=PERMUT(B2,B3)
8	1 in about 10 billion chance of winning	
9		
10	**Arrangement Not Important**	
11	**Possible Outcomes**	**Formula**
12	13,983,816	=COMBIN(B2,B3)
13	1 in about 14 million chance of winning	

Video Available: Watch the Chapter 4—Counting Video

Probability Distributions: Definitions

A probability distribution gives the entire range of values that can occur based on an experiment. A probability distribution is similar to a relative frequency distribution. However, instead of describing the past, it describes a likely future event. For example, a drug manufacturer may claim a treatment will cause weight loss for 80% of the population. A consumer protection agency may test the treatment on a sample of six people. If the manufacturer's claim is true, it is almost impossible to have an outcome where no one in the sample loses weight and it is most likely that five out of the six do lose weight.

Basic Definitions

- **Probability distribution** is a listing of all the outcomes of an experiment and the probability associated with each outcome.
  - The probability of a particular outcome is between 0 and 1 inclusive.
  - The outcomes are mutually exclusive events.
  - The list is exhaustive so the sum of the probabilities of the various events is equal to 1.
- **Random variable** is a quantity resulting from an experiment that, by chance, can assume different values.
  - **Discrete random variable** is a random variable that can assume only certain clearly separated values. It is usually the result of things that can be counted.
    - Types: **Binomial, Hypergeometric, and Poisson**
  - **Continuous random variable** can assume an infinite number of values within a given range. It is usually the result of things that can be measured.
    - Types: **Uniform, Normal, and Exponential**
  - Trials are **independent** if the occurrence of one trial does not affect the occurrence of another. One way to think about independence is to assume that trials A and B occur at different times. For example, when trial B occurs after trial A occurs, does A have any effect on the likelihood that trial B occurs? If the answer is no, then the trials are independent.

FIGURE 3 Probability Distribution Decision Tree

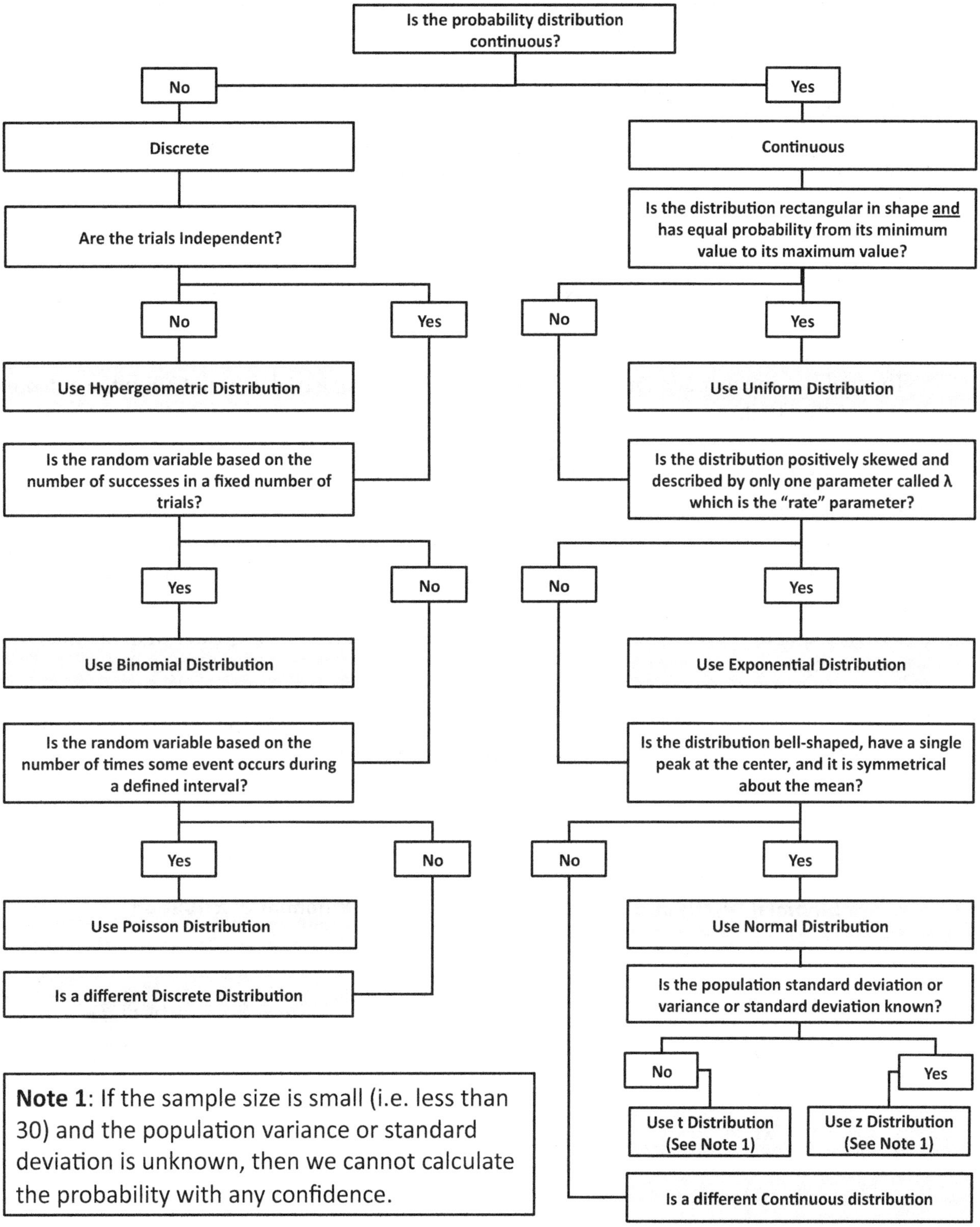

The Binomial Probability Distribution

Characterized By

- Random variable is discrete and a result of counts.
- The trials are independent.
- The random variable counts the number of successes in a fixed number of trials.
- There are only two possible outcomes on a particular trial of an experiment.
- The outcomes are mutually exclusive.

In a Binomial Probability Experiment

- An outcome on each trial of an experiment is classified into one of two mutually exclusive categories—a success or failure.
- The probability of success and failure stay the same for each trial.
- The trials are independent, meaning that the outcome of one trial does not affect the outcome of any other trial.

Calculating Probabilities Using a Binomial Distribution

First, identify the correct case per Figures 4 through 6

- Use case A to find probabilities where the number of occurrences exactly equals a given value.
- Use case B to find probabilities where the number of occurrences is less than or equal to a given value.
- Use case C to find probabilities where the number of occurrences is greater than or equal to a given value.

Next, implement the correct Excel function according to Table 2 and using the correct case identified above. **Please note that the black bars indicate probability areas.**

FIGURE 4
Case A: Keyword—Exactly

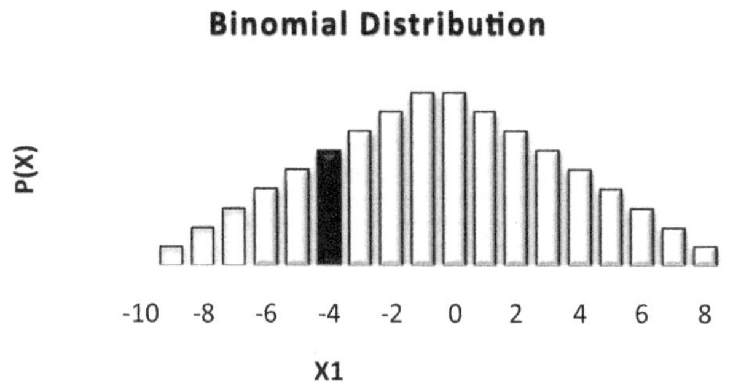

FIGURE 5
Case B: Keyword—Less Than or Equal To

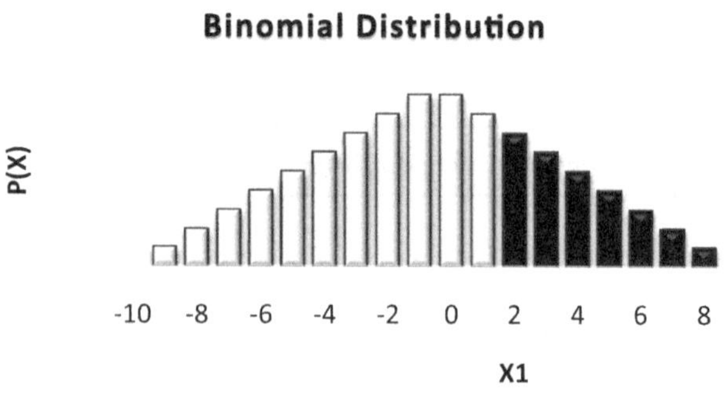

FIGURE 6 Case C: Greater Than or Equal To

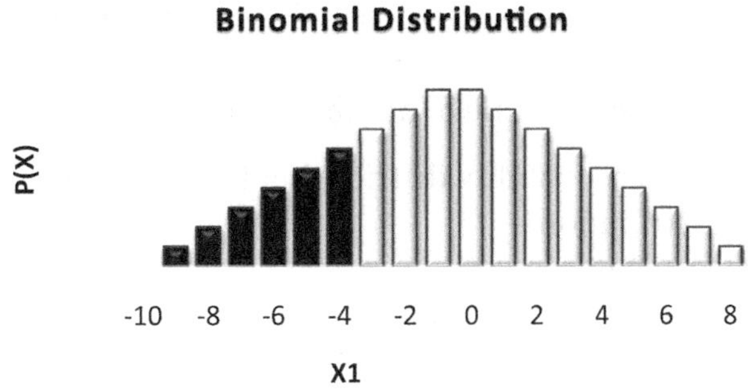

TABLE 2 Binomial Distribution Formulas

Binomial Distribution Formulas		
Result	Case—Keyword	Excel Formula
Probability P(x = X1)	Case A: Exactly	=BINOM.DIST(X1,n,p,false)
Probability P(x <= X1)	Case B: Less than or equal to	=BINOM.DIST(X1,n,p,true)
Probability P(x >= X1)	Case C: Greater than or equal to	=1-BINOM.DIST(X1-1,n,p,true)
Mean	All	$\mu = np$
Variance	All	$\sigma^2 = np(1-p)$
Standard Deviation	All	$\sigma = \sqrt{np(1-p)}$

Where:

- X1 defines the value or boundary of the probability area
- n is the random sample size (number of trials)
- p is the probability of success (probability_s)
- x is the random variable, the number of successes in the random sample
- μ is the mean
- σ^2 is the variance
- σ is the standard deviation

Binomial Probability Distribution Example Problem

An auditor audits six returns per day and finds errors on 40% of these returns. Use a three-day time period as a basis to complete the following tasks (successful audits = errors found). The trials are assumed to be independent because of the huge number of auditable returns available for review.

a. Identify the correct type of probability distribution for this case
b. Build the probability distribution
c. Build the cumulative distribution
d. Graph the probability and cumulative distribution
e. Find the probability that exactly 5 returns with errors are found
f. Find the probability that 6 or less returns with errors are found
g. Find the probability that 5 or more returns with errors are found
h. Find the mean number of successful audits
i. Find the standard deviation of successful audits

TABLE 3 Binomial Probability Distribution Solution Example

	A	B	C
1	**Information Given in Problem**		
2	Random Sample Size	n	18
3	Probability of Success	p	40.0%
4			
5	**a. Decision Tree**		
6	Is the probability distribution continuous?	No	
7	Are the trials independent?	Yes	
8	Is this a rate problem?	No	
9	Binomial Distribution		
10			
11	**# of audits**	**b. Probability**	**c. Cumulative Distribution**
12	0	0.0%	0.0%
13	1	0.1%	0.1%
14	2	0.7%	0.8%
15	3	2.5%	3.3%
16	4	6.1%	9.4%
17	5	11.5%	20.9%
18	6	16.6%	37.4%
19	7	18.9%	56.3%
20	8	17.3%	73.7%

21	9	12.8%	86.5%
22	10	7.7%	94.2%
23	11	3.7%	98.0%
24	12	1.5%	99.4%
25	13	0.4%	99.9%
26	14	0.1%	100.0%
27			
28	b. Probability Distribution Function (cell B12)	=BINOM.DIST(A12,$C$2,$C$3,FALSE)	
29	c. Cumulative Distribution Function (cell C12)	=BINOM.DIST(A12,$C$2,$C$3,TRUE)	
30	d. Graph the probability distribution	See chart	
31	e. Exactly 5 returns	11.5%	=BINOM.DIST(5,C2,C3,FALSE)
32	f. 6 or less returns	37.4%	=BINOM.DIST(6,C2,C3,TRUE)
33	g. 5 or more returns	90.6%	=1-BINOM.DIST(5-1,C2,C3,TRUE)
34	h. Mean	7.2	=C2*C3
35	i. Standard Deviation	2.1	=SQRT(C2*C3*(1-C3))

FIGURE 7 Binomial Probability With Cumulative Probability Distribution Example

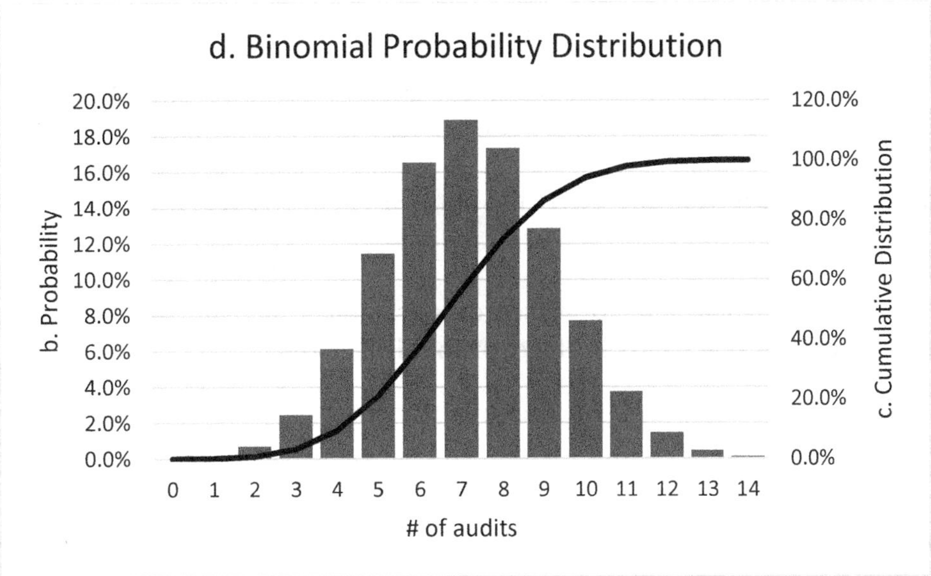

Video Available: Watch the Chapter 4—Binomial Distribution Video

Hypergeometric Probability Distribution

Characterized By

- Random variable is discrete and a result of counts.
- The trials are NOT independent.
- The random variable counts the number of successes in a fixed number of trials.
- There are only two possible outcomes on a particular trial of an experiment.
- The outcomes are mutually exclusive.

In a Hypergeometric Probability Experiment

- An outcome on each trial of an experiment is classified into one of two mutually exclusive categories—a success or failure.
- The random variable counts the number of successes in a fixed number of trials.
- The trials are dependent, meaning that the outcome of one trial affects the outcome of the next trial.
- Use hypergeometric distribution if experiment is binomial, but sampling is without replacement from a finite population where n/N is more than 0.05

Calculating Probabilities Using a Hypergeometric Distribution

First, identify the correct case per Figures 8 through 10

- Use case A to find probabilities where the number of occurrences exactly equals a given value.
- Use case B to find probabilities where the number of occurrences is less than or equal to a given value.
- Use case C to find probabilities where the number of occurrences is greater than or equal to a given value.

Next, implement the correct Excel function according to Table 4 and using the correct case identified above. **Please note that the black bars indicate probability areas.**

FIGURE 8
Case A: Keyword—Exactly

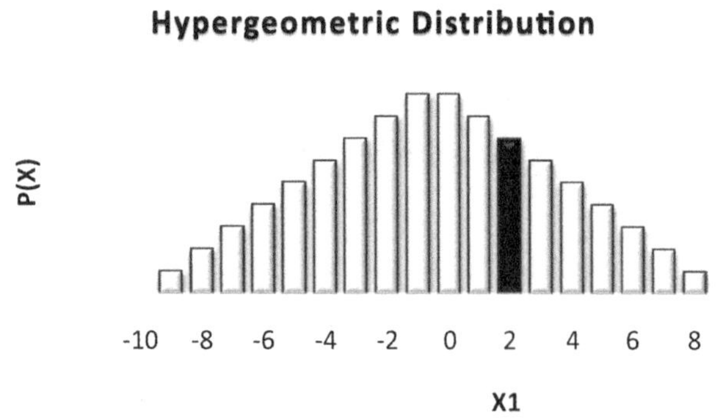

FIGURE 9
Case B: Keyword—Less Than or Equal To

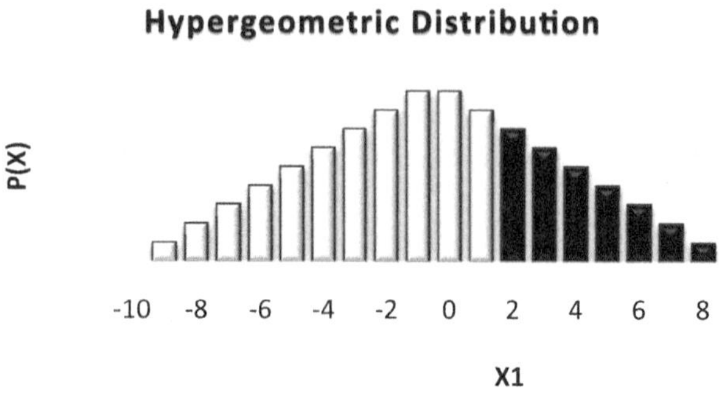

FIGURE 10 Case C: Keyword—Greater Than or Equal To

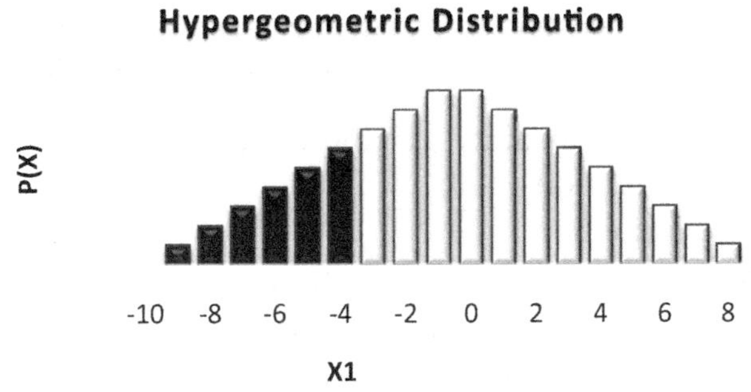

TABLE 4 Hypergeometric Distribution Formulas

Hypergeometric Distribution Formulas		
Result	**Case—Keyword**	**Excel Formula**
Probability P(x = X1)	Case A: Exactly	=HYPGEOM.DIST(X1,n,k,N,false)
Probability P(x <= X1)	Case B: Less than or equal to	=HYPGEOM.DIST((X1,n,k,N,true)
Probability P(x >= X1)	Case C: Greater than or equal to	=1-HYPGEOM.DIST(X1-1,n,k,N,true)
Mean	All	$\mu = \frac{nk}{N}$
Variance	All	$\sigma^2 = \frac{nk(N-k)(N-n)}{N^2(N-1)}$
Standard Deviation	All	$\sigma = \sqrt{\frac{nk(N-k)(N-n)}{N^2(N-1)}}$

Where:

- x is the random variable, the number of successes in the random sample (sample_s)
- n is the random sample size (number_sample)
- k is the number of successes in the population (population_s)
- N is the size of the population (num_pop)
- μ is the mean
- σ^2 is the variance
- σ is the standard deviation
- X1 defines the value or boundary of the probability area
- Note: Excel doesn't provide an inverse function for the Hypergeometric Distribution

Hypergeometric Probability Distribution Example Problem

Jim's Bakery has 18 delivery trucks, used mainly to deliver fresh bread to local grocery stores. Of these 18 trucks, 8 have electrical issues. A sample of 10 trucks is randomly selected.

a. Identify the correct type of probability distribution for this case
b. Build the probability distribution
c. Build the cumulative distribution
d. Graph the probability and cumulative distribution
e. Find the probability that exactly 5 trucks will have electrical issues
f. Find the probability that 6 or less trucks will have electrical issues
g. Find the probability that 5 or more trucks will have electrical issues
h. Find the mean number of trucks with electrical issues
i. Find the standard deviation of trucks with electrical issues

TABLE 5 Hypergeometric Probability Distribution Solution Example

	A	B	C
1	**Information Given in Problem**		
2	Random Sample Size	n	10
3	Successes in Population	k	8
4	Size of the Population	N	18
5			
6	**a. Decision Tree**		
7	Is the probability distribution continuous?	No	
8	Are the trials independent?	No	
9	Is this a rate problem?	N/A	
10	Hypergeometric Distribution		
11			
12	**Trucks with Electrical Issues (x)**	**b. Probability**	**c. Cumulative Distribution**
13	0	0.0%	0.0%
14	1	0.2%	0.2%
15	2	2.9%	3.1%
16	3	15.4%	18.4%
17	4	33.6%	52.0%
18	5	32.3%	84.3%
19	6	13.4%	97.7%
20	7	2.2%	99.9%
21	8	0.1%	100.0%
22			

23	b. Probability Distribution Function (cell B13)	=HYPGEOM.DIST(A13,$C$2,$C$3,$C$4,FALSE)	
24	c. Cumulative Distribution Function (cell C13)	=HYPGEOM.DIST(A13,$C$2,$C$3,$C$4,TRUE)	
25	d. Graph the probability distribution	See chart	
26	e. Exactly 5 trucks	32.3%	=HYPGEOM.DIST(5,$C$2,$C$3,$C$4,FALSE)
27	f. 6 or less trucks	97.7%	=HYPGEOM.DIST(6,$C$2,$C$3,$C$4,TRUE)
28	g. 5 or more trucks	48.0%	=1-HYPGEOM.DIST(5-1,$C$2,$C$3,$C$4,TRUE)
29	h. Mean	4.44	=(C2*C3)/C4
30	i. Standard Deviation	1.1	=SQRT(C2*C3*(C4-C3)*(C4-C2)/(C4^2*(C4-1)))

FIGURE 11 Hypergeometric Probability and Cumulative Probability Distributions Example

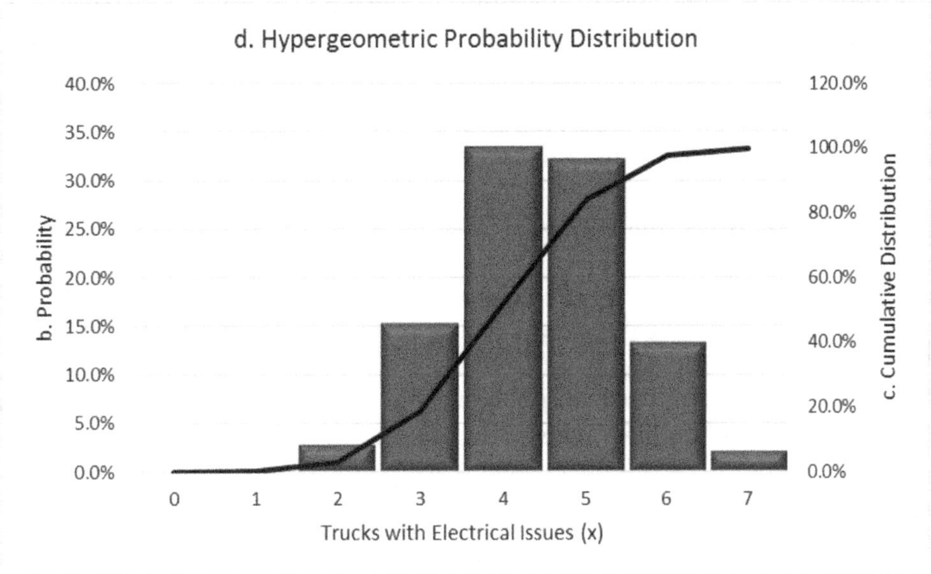

Video Available: Watch the Chapter 4—Hypergeometric Distribution Video

Poisson Probability Distribution

Characterized By

- **Random variable is discrete and a result of counts.**
- **The trials are independent.**
- **The random variable counts the number of successes during a specified interval.**
- There are only two possible outcomes on a particular trial of an experiment.
- The outcomes are mutually exclusive.

In a Poisson Probability Experiment

- The random variable is the number of times some event occurs during a defined interval, which can be described as a rate. The interval arrival unit may be time, distance, area, or volume.
- The Poisson probability distribution is always positively skewed and the random variable has no specific upper limit.
- As μ becomes larger, the Poisson distribution becomes more symmetrical (i.e., approaches "bell shaped").

Applications

- Number of imperfections in a manufacturing process
- Number of defective parts in outgoing shipments
- Number of customers waiting in line

Calculating Probabilities Using a Poisson Distribution

First, identify the correct case per Figures 12 through 14.

- Use case A to find probabilities where the number of occurrences exactly equals a given value.
- Use case B to find probabilities where the number of occurrences is less than or equal to a given value.
- Use case C to find probabilities where the number of occurrences is greater than or equal to a given value.

Next, implement the correct Excel function according to Table 6 and using the correct case identified above. **Please note black bars indicate probability areas.**

FIGURE 12
Case A: Keyword—Exactly

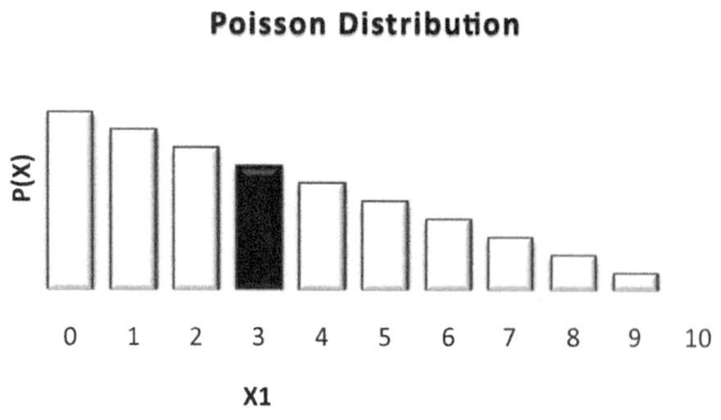

FIGURE 13
Case B: Keyword—Less Than or Equal To

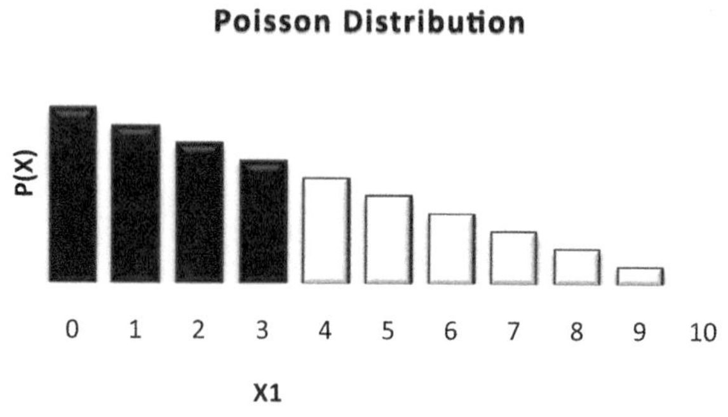

FIGURE 14 Case C: Greater Than or Equal To

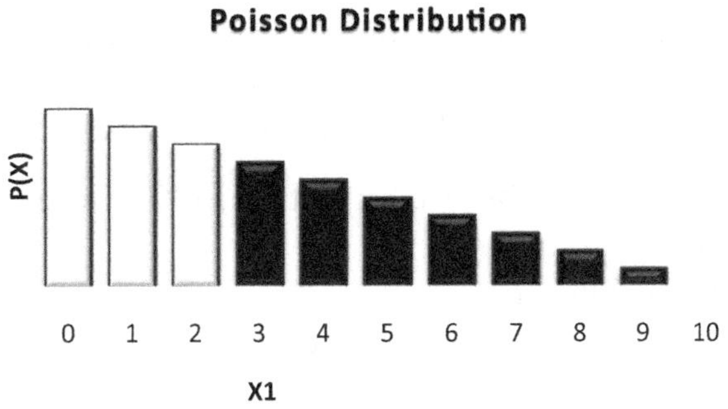

TABLE 6 Poisson Distribution Formulas

Poisson Distribution Formulas		
Result	**Case - Keyword**	**Excel Formula**
Probability P(x = X1)	Case A: Exactly	=POISSON.DIST(X1,μ,false)
Probability P(x <= X1)	Case B: Less than or equal to	=POISSON.DIST((X1,μ,true)
Probability P(x >= X1)	Case C: Greater than or equal to	=1-POISSON.DIST(X1-1,μ,true)
Mean	All	$\mu = n\pi$
Variance	All	$\sigma^2 = \mu$
Standard Deviation	All	$\sigma = \sqrt{\mu}$

Where:

- x is the random variable, the number of successes in the random sample
- n is the total number of trials
- π is the probability
- μ is the mean
- X1 is the boundary of the probability area

Poisson Probability Distribution Example Problem

It is estimated that 3 calls per day to the Customer Service department of ATT will wait more than 15 minutes and on an average day they receive 1,050 calls. Therefore, the probability that a caller will wait more than 15 minutes is 3/1050. Today they received 950 calls.

a. Identify the correct type of probability distribution for this case
b. Build the probability distribution
c. Build the cumulative distribution
d. Graph the probability and cumulative distribution
e. Find the probability that exactly 5 calls will have a wait time > 15 minutes
f. Find the probability that 6 or less calls will have a wait time > 15 minutes
g. Find the probability that 5 or more calls will have a wait time > 15 minutes
h. Find the mean number of truck calls with a wait time > 15 minutes
i. Find the standard deviation of calls with a wait time > 15 minutes

TABLE 7 Poisson Probability Distribution Solution Example

	A	B	C
1	**Information Given in Problem**		
2	Random Sample Size	n	950
3	Probability	π	0.29%
4	Calculated Mean	π = nπ	2.7
5			
6	**a. Decision Tree**		
7	Is the probability distribution continuous?	No	
8	Are the trials independent?	Yes	
9	Is this a rate problem?	Yes	
10	Poisson Distribution		
11			
12	**Calls With Wait Time > 15 minutes (x)**	**b. Probability**	**c. Cumulative Distribution**
13	0	6.6%	6.6%
14	1	18.0%	24.6%
15	2	24.4%	49.0%
16	3	22.1%	71.1%
17	4	15.0%	86.1%
18	5	8.1%	94.2%
19	6	3.7%	97.9%

20	7	1.4%	99.3%
21	8	0.5%	99.8%
22	9	0.1%	99.9%
23	10	0.0%	100.0%
24			
25	b. Probability Distribution Function (cell B13)	=POISSON.DIST($A13,$C$4,FALSE)	
26	c. Cumulative Distribution Function (cell C13)	=POISSON.DIST($A13,$C$4,TRUE)	
27	d. Graph the probability distribution	See chart	
28	e. Exactly 5 calls	8.1%	=POISSON.DIST(5,C4,FALSE)
29	f. 6 or less calls	97.9%	=POISSON.DIST(6,C4,TRUE)
30	g. 5 or more calls	13.9%	=1-POISSON.DIST(5-1,C4,TRUE)
31	h. Mean	2.7	=C2*C3
32	i. Standard Deviation	1.6	=SQRT(C2*C3)

FIGURE 15 Poisson Probability and Cumulative Probability Distribution Chart

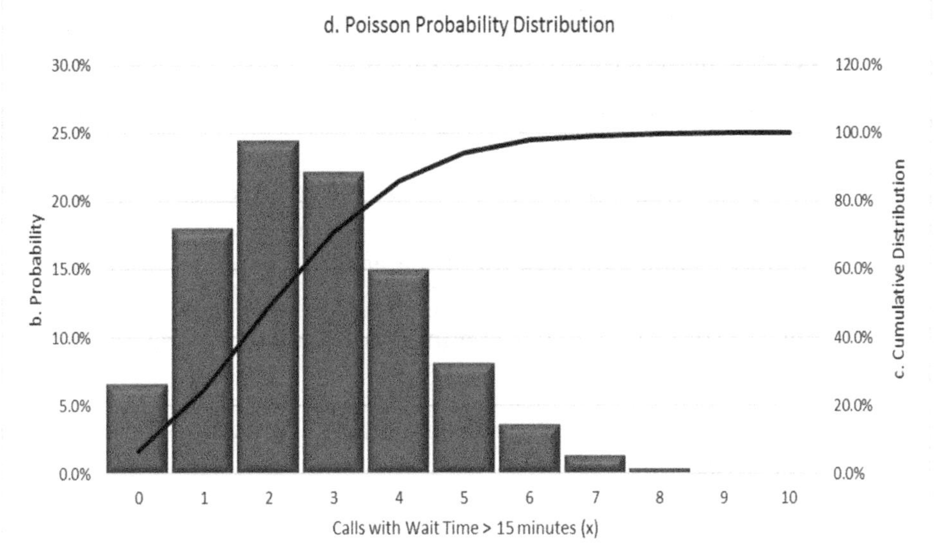

Video Available: Watch the Chapter 4—Poisson Distribution Video

Uniform Probability Distribution

Characterized By

- Random variable is continuous
- The distribution is rectangular in shape and has equal probability from its minimum value to its maximum value

In a Uniform Probability Experiment

- The uniform probability distribution is rectangular in shape and is completely defined by its minimum and maximum values.
- The probability is the same across the entire distribution.
- The mean of a uniform distribution is located in the middle of the interval between the minimum (a) and maximum (b) values.

Applications

- Sales over a given time
- Time required to complete a task

Calculating Probabilities Using a Uniform Distribution

First, identify the correct case per Figures 16 through 19.

- Use case A to find probabilities where the number of occurrences is less than to a given value (X1).
- Use case B to find probabilities where the number of occurrences is greater than to a given value (X1).
- Use case C to find probabilities where the number of occurrences is greater than to a given value (X1) and less than another given value (X2).
- Use case D to find probabilities where the number of occurrences is less than to a given value (X1) or greater than another given value (X2).

Next, implement the correct Excel function according to Table 8 and using the correct case identified above. **Black bars indicate probability areas.**

FIGURE 16
Case A: Keyword—Less Than X1

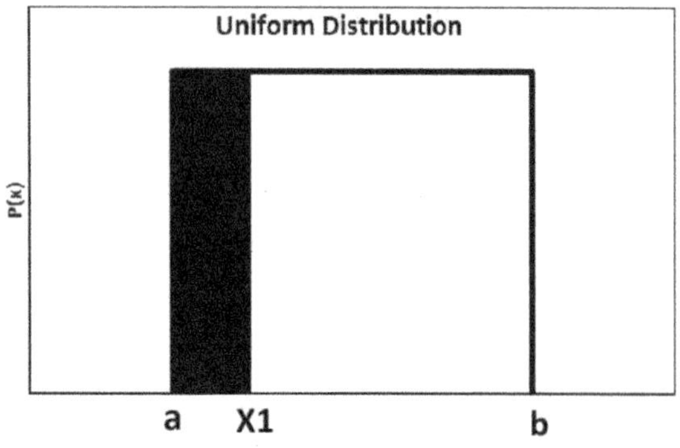

FIGURE 17
Case B: Keyword—Greater Than X1

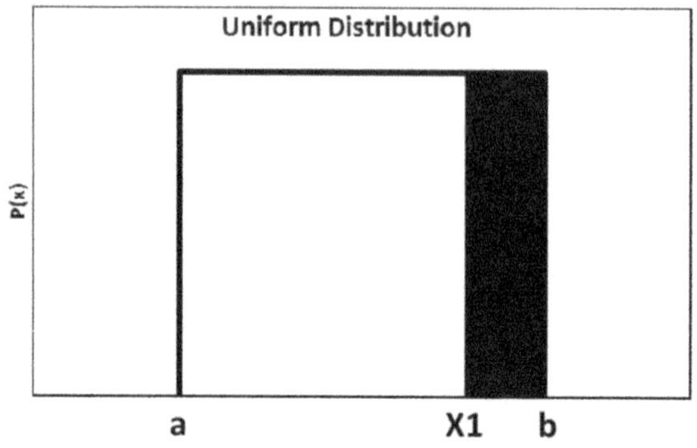

FIGURE 18
Case C: Keyword—Between X1 and X2

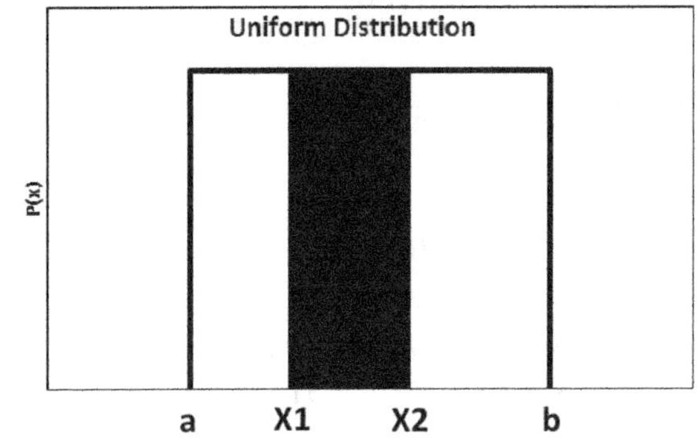

FIGURE 19
Case A: Keyword—Less Than X1 or Greater Than X2

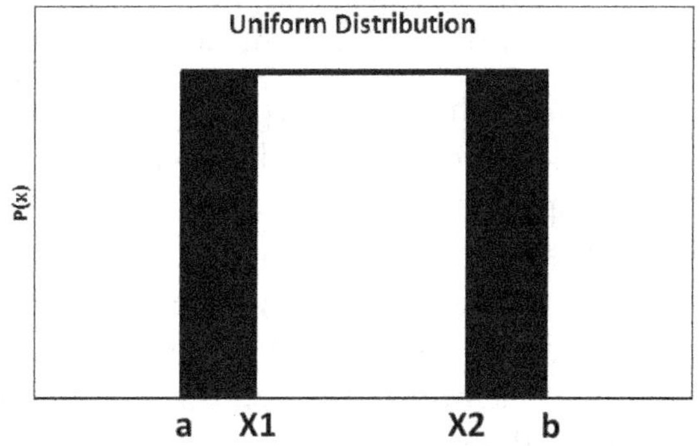

TABLE 8 Uniform Distribution Formulas

Uniform Distribution Formulas		
Result	**Case—Keyword**	**Excel Formula**
Probability $P(x < X1)$	Case A: Less than	$=\frac{X1-a}{b-a}$
Probability $P(x > X1)$	Case B: Greater than	$=1-\frac{X1-a}{b-a}$
Probability $P(X1 < x < X2)$	Case C: Between	$=\frac{X2-X1}{b-a}$
Probability $P(x < X1 \text{ or } x > X2)$	Case D: Less than OR Greater than	$=\frac{X1-a}{b-a}+1-\frac{X2-a}{b-a}$
Mean	All	$\mu=\frac{a+b}{2}$
Standard Deviation	All	$\sigma=\sqrt{\frac{(b-a)(b-a)^2}{12}}$

Where:

- a is the minimum value in the distribution
- b is the maximum value in the distribution
- x is the random variable
- X1 and X2 are the boundaries of the probability areas

Uniform Probability Distribution Example Problem

According to USAA, a family of four spends between $400 and $4,400 per year on all types of insurance. Suppose the money spent is uniformly distributed between these amounts. For the probability questions, assume we select one family at random.

a. Identify the correct type of probability distribution for this case
b. Build the cumulative distribution
c. Graph the cumulative distribution
d. Find the probability that the money spent per family is < $1,400
e. Find the probability that the money spent per family is > $1,400
f. Find the probability that the money spent per family is > $1,400 and < $1,900
g. Find the probability that the money spent per family is < $1,400 or > $1,900
h. Find the mean money spent per family
i. Find the standard deviation of the money spent per family

TABLE 9 Uniform Probability Distribution Solution Example

	A	B	C
1	**Information Given in Problem**		
2	Minimum Value	a	$400.00
3	Maximum Value	b	$4,400.00
4			
5	**a. Decision Tree**		
6	Is the probability distribution continuous	Yes	
7	Are the probabilities equal	Yes	
8	Uniform Distribution		
9			
10	**Money spent per family**	**c. Cumulative Distribution**	
11	$400	0.0%	
12	$900	12.5%	
13	$1,400	25.0%	
14	$1,900	37.5%	
15	$2,400	50.0%	
16	$2,900	62.5%	
17	$3,400	75.0%	
18	$3,900	87.5%	
19	$4,400	100.0%	
20			

21	b. Cumulative Distribution Function (cell B11)	=(A11-$C$2)/($C$3-$C$2)	
22	c. Graph the probability distribution	See chart	
23	d. The money spent per family is < $1,400	25.0%	=(1400-C2)/(C3-C2)
24	e. Money spent per family is > $1,400	75.0%	=1-(1400-C2)/(C3-C2)
25	f. Money spent per family is > $1,400 and < $1,900	12.5%	=(1900-1400)/(C3-C2)
26	g. Money spent per family is < $1,400 or > $1,900	87.5%	=(1400-$C$2)/(C3-C2)+(1-(1900-C2)/(C3-C2))
27	h. Mean	$2,400	=(C3+C2)/2
28	i. Standard Deviation	$1,154.70	=SQRT((C3-C2)^2/12)

FIGURE 20 Uniform Probability and Cumulative Probability Distribution Example

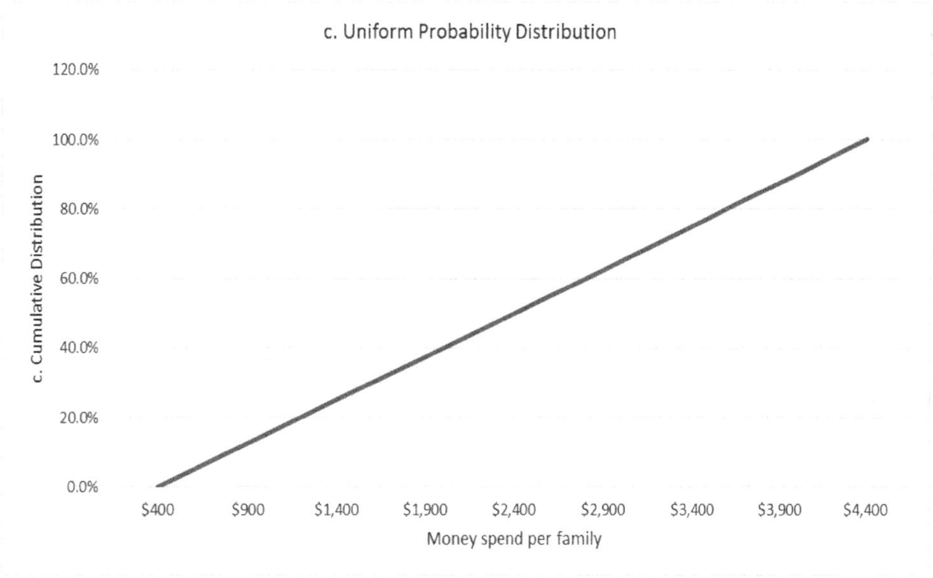

Video Available: Watch the Chapter 4—Uniform Distribution Video

Exponential Probability Distribution

Characterized By

- Random variable is continuous.
- Described by only one parameter, which we identify as λ, often referred to as the "rate" of occurrence parameter.
- Positively skewed, similar to the Poisson distribution (for discrete variables).
- Not symmetric like the uniform and normal distributions.
- As λ decreases, the shape of the distribution becomes "less skewed."

Applications

- Product Reliability—time to failure and rate of failure
- Service times and queue lengths

Calculating Probabilities Using an Exponential Distribution

First, identify the correct case per Figures 21 through 24

- Use case A to find probabilities where the number of occurrences is less than to a given value (X1).
- Use case B to find probabilities where the number of occurrences is greater than to a given value (X1).
- Use case C to find probabilities where the number of occurrences is greater than to a given value (X1) and less than another given value (X2).
- Use case D to find probabilities where the number of occurrences is less than to a given value (X1) or greater than another given value (X2).

Next, implement the correct Excel function according to Table 10 and using the correct case identified above. **Please note black bars indicate probability areas.**

FIGURE 21 Case A: Keyword—Less Than X1

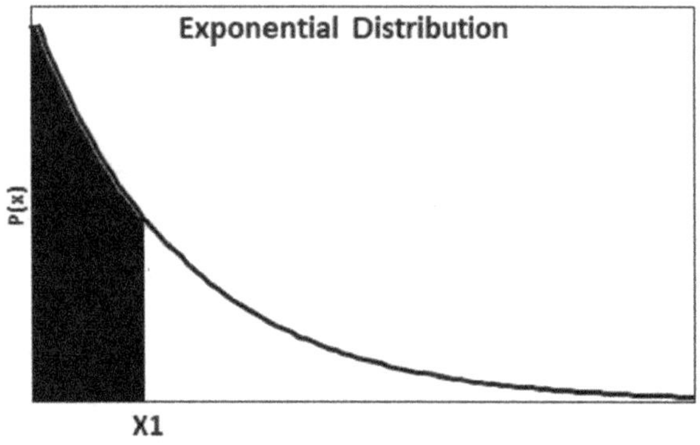

FIGURE 22 Case B: Keyword—Greater Than X1

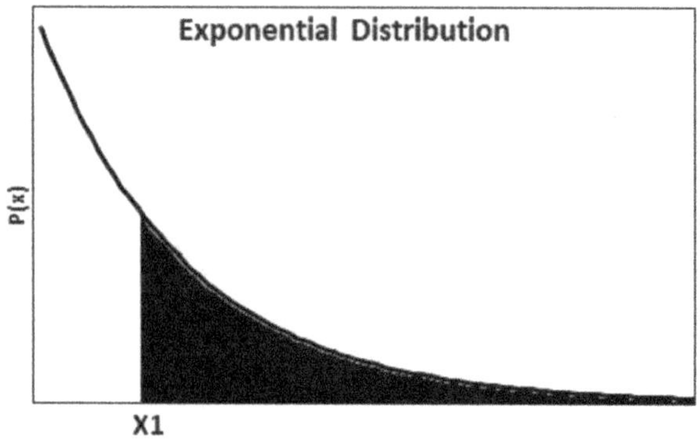

FIGURE 23 Case C: Keyword—Between X1 and X2

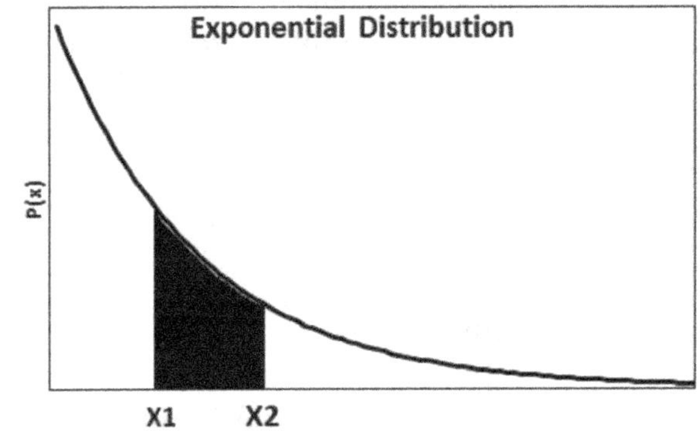

FIGURE 24 Case D: Keyword—Less Than X1 or Greater Than X2

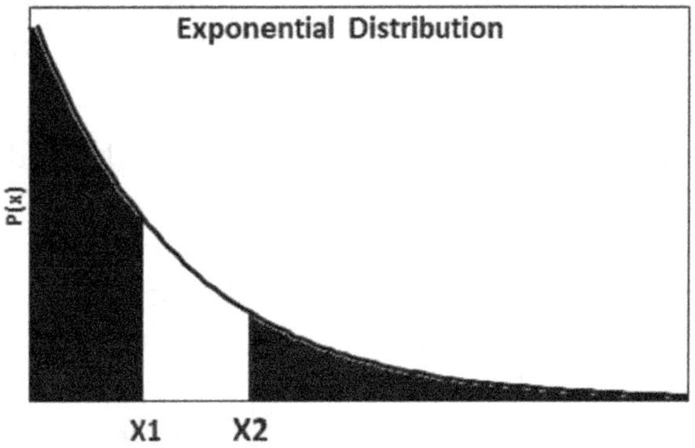

TABLE 10 Exponential Distribution Formulas

Exponential Distribution Formulas		
Result	**Case—Keyword**	**Excel Formula**
Probability P(x < X1)	Case A: Less than	=EXPON.DIST(X1,λ,TRUE)
Probability P(x > X1)	Case B: Greater than	=1-EXPON.DIST(X1,λ,TRUE)
Probability P(X1 < x < X2)	Case C: Between	=EXPON.DIST(X2,λ,TRUE)-EXPON.DIST(X1,λ,TRUE)
Probability P(x < X1 or x > X2)	Case D: Less than OR Greater than	=1-EXPON.DIST(X2,λ,TRUE)+EXPON.DIST(X1,λ,TRUE)
Mean	All	$\mu=\lambda^{-1}$
Standard Deviation	All	σ=SQRT(λ^{-2})

Where:

- λ is lambda, the population parameter
- x is the random variable
- X1 and X2 are the limits of the probability areas
- Note: Excel doesn't provide an inverse function for the Exponential Distribution

Exponential Probability Distribution Example Problem

Students arrive at a local bar according to an approximate Poisson process at a mean rate of 30 students per hour. What is the probability that the bouncer has to wait more than 3 minutes to card the next student?

a. Identify the correct type of probability distribution for this case
b. Build the probability distribution
c. Build the cumulative distribution
d. Graph the cumulative distribution
e. Find the probability that the time between carding is < 3 minutes
f. Find the probability that the time between carding is > 3 minutes
g. Find the probability that the time between carding is between 3 minutes and 5 minutes
h. Find the probability that the time between carding is less than 3 minutes or greater than 5 minutes
i. Find the mean time between carding
j. Find the standard deviation of time between carding

TABLE 11 Exponential Probability Distribution Solution Example

	A	B	C
1	**Information Given in Problem**		
2	Arrival Rate (30 students/hour)	λ (students/minute)	0.50
3			
4	**a. Decision Tree**		
5	Is the probability distribution continuous	Yes	
6	Are the probabilities equal	No	
7	Is the distribution described by the rate	Yes	
8	Exponential		
9			
10	**Wait time between students (min)**	**b. Probability Distribution**	**c. Cumulative Distribution**
11	0.5	38.9%	22.1%
12	1.0	30.3%	39.3%
13	1.5	23.6%	52.8%
14	2.0	18.4%	63.2%
15	2.5	14.3%	71.3%
16	3.0	11.2%	77.7%
17	3.5	8.7%	82.6%
18	4.0	6.8%	86.5%
19	4.5	5.3%	89.5%

20	5.0	4.1%	91.8%
21	5.5	3.2%	93.6%
22	6.0	2.5%	95.0%
23	6.5	1.9%	96.1%
24	7.0	1.5%	97.0%
25	7.5	1.2%	97.6%
26			
27	b. Probability Distribution Function (cell B11)	=EXPON.DIST(A11,$C$2,FALSE)	
28	c. Cumulative Distribution Function (cell C11)	=EXPON.DIST(A11,$C$2,TRUE)	
29	d. Graph the probability distribution	See chart	
30	e. Time between carding < 3 min	77.7%	=EXPON.DIST(3,C2,TRUE)
31	f. Time between carding > 3 min	22.3%	=1-EXPON.DIST(3,C2,TRUE)
32	g. Time between carding between 3 and 5 min	14.1%	=EXPON.DIST(5,C2,TRUE)-EXPON.DIST(3,C2,TRUE)
33	h. Time between carding < 3 min or > 5 min	85.9%	=1-EXPON.DIST(5,C2,TRUE)+ EXPON.DIST(3,C2,TRUE)
34	h. Mean	2.00	=C2^-1
35	i. Standard Deviation	2.00	=SQRT(C2^-2)

FIGURE 25 Exponential Probability and Cumulative Probability Example

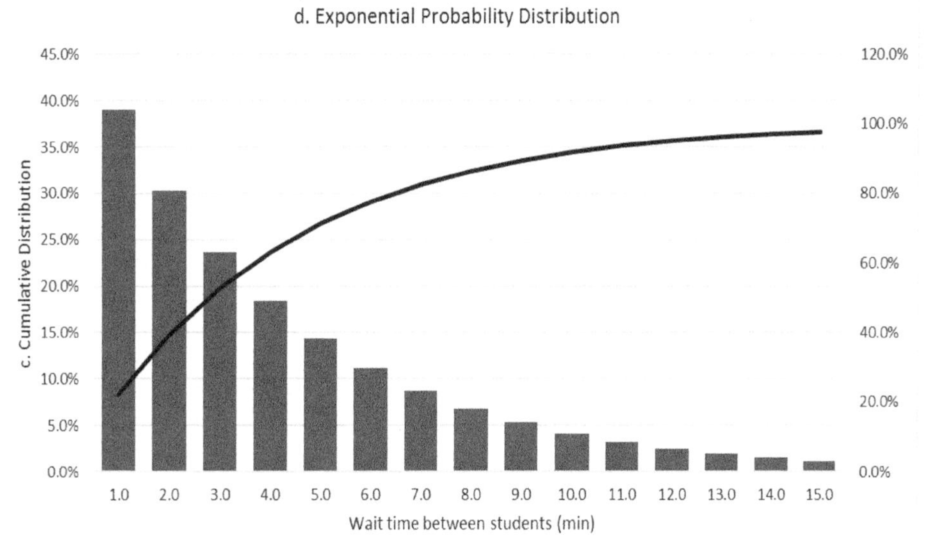

Sampling Methods

Basic Definitions

- A probability sample is a sample selected such that each item or person in the population being studied has a known likelihood of being included in the sample.
- Sampling Error is the difference between a sample statistic and its corresponding population parameter.
- The sampling distribution of the sample mean is a probability distribution consisting of all possible sample means of a given sample size selected from a population.

Types of Probability Sampling Methods

- Simple Random Sample: A sample selected so that each item or person in the population has the same chance of being included.
- Systematic Random Sampling: The items or individuals of the population are arranged in some order. A random starting point is selected and then every kth member of the population is selected for the sample.
- Stratified Random Sampling: A population is first divided into subgroups, called strata, and a sample is selected from each stratum. Useful when a population can be clearly divided in groups based on some characteristics.
- Cluster Sampling: A population is divided into clusters using naturally occurring geographic or other boundaries. Then, clusters are randomly selected and a sample is collected by randomly selecting from each cluster.

Central Limit Theorem (CLT)

CLT Textbook Definition: If all samples of a particular size are selected from any population, the sampling distribution of the sample mean is approximately a normal distribution. This approximation improves with larger samples. (Lind, 2015)

If the population follows a normal probability distribution, then for any sample size the sampling distribution of the sample mean will also be normal. If the population distribution is symmetrical (but not normal), the normal shape of the distribution of the sample mean emerges with samples as **small as 10**. If a distribution is skewed or has thick tails, it may require samples of 30 or more to observe the normality feature.

Implication: We can use well-developed statistical inference procedures that are based on a normal distribution, even if we are sampling from a population that is not normal, provided we have a large enough sample size. Sample sizes of 30 or larger are adequate in most situations and so we will use sample sizes of 30 or larger to apply the central limit theorem for this text.

Some applications of the CLT are

- Estimating probabilities
- Finding confidence intervals
- Conducting hypothesis testing

Standard Error of the Mean (SE)

- Is defined by $SE = \frac{\sigma}{\sqrt{n}}$
- The mean of the distribution of sample means will be exactly equal to the population mean if we are able to select all possible samples of the same size from a given population.
- There will be less dispersion in the sampling distribution of the sample mean than in the population. As the sample size increases, the standard error of the mean decreases.

Video Available: Watch the Chapter 4—Normal CLT Distribution Video

Normal Probability Distribution

The Normal Probability Distribution Is the Most Widely Used Form of Continuous Probability Distribution and Is Characterized By:

- It is bell-shaped and has a single peak at the center of the distribution.
- It is symmetrical about the mean.
- It is asymptotic: The curve gets closer and closer to the X-axis but never actually touches it. To put it another way, the tails of the curve extend indefinitely in both directions.
- The location of a normal distribution is determined by the mean (μ), the dispersion or spread of the distribution is determined by the standard deviation (σ).
- The arithmetic mean, median, and mode are equal.
- The total area under the curve is 1.00; half the area under the normal curve is to the right of this center point, the mean, and the other half to the left of it.

The Standard Normal Probability Distribution

- Is a normal distribution with a mean of 0 and a standard deviation of 1.
- It is also called the z-distribution.

Empirical Rule

- About 68% of the area under the normal curve is within one standard deviation of the mean.
- About 95% is within two standard deviations of the mean.
- Practically all is within three standard deviations of the mean.

Normal Approximation to the Binomial

- The normal distribution (a continuous distribution) yields a good approximation of the binomial distribution (a discrete distribution) for large values of n.
- The normal probability distribution is generally a good approximation to the binomial probability distribution when $n\pi$ and $n(1-\pi)$ are both greater than 5.
- The value .5 subtracted or added, depending on the problem, to a selected value when a binomial probability distribution (a discrete probability distribution) is being approximated by a continuous probability distribution (the normal distribution).
- Only one of four cases may arise:
  - For the probability at least X occurs, use the area above (X -.5).
  - For the probability that more than X occurs, use the area above (X+.5).
  - For the probability that X or fewer occurs, use the area below (X -.5).
  - For the probability that fewer than X occurs, use the area below (X+.5).

Calculating Probabilities Using a Normal Distribution

First, identify the correct case per Figures 26 through 29

- Use case A to find probabilities where the number of occurrences is less than to a given value (X1).
- Use case B to find probabilities where the number of occurrences is greater than to a given value (X1).
- Use case C to find probabilities where the number of occurrences is greater than to a given value (X1) and less than another given value (X2).
- Use case D to find probabilities where the number of occurrences is less than to a given value (X1) or greater than another given value (X2).

Next, implement the correct Excel function according to Table 12 or Table 13 depending on whether the population standard deviation is known or unknown and using the correct case identified above. **Please note black bars indicate probability areas.**

FIGURE 26 Case A: Keyword—Less Than X1

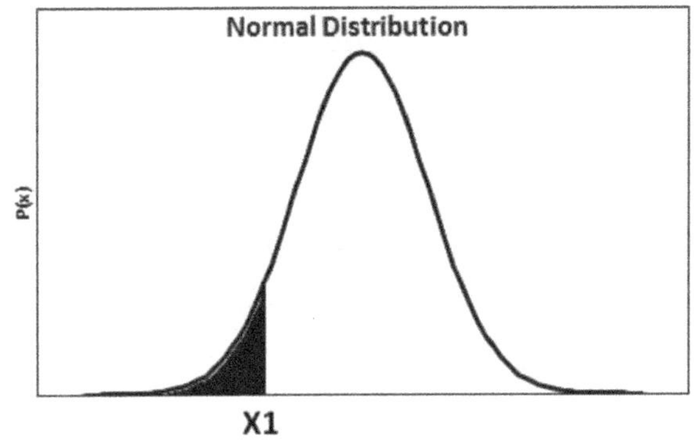

FIGURE 27 Case B: Keyword—Greater Than X1

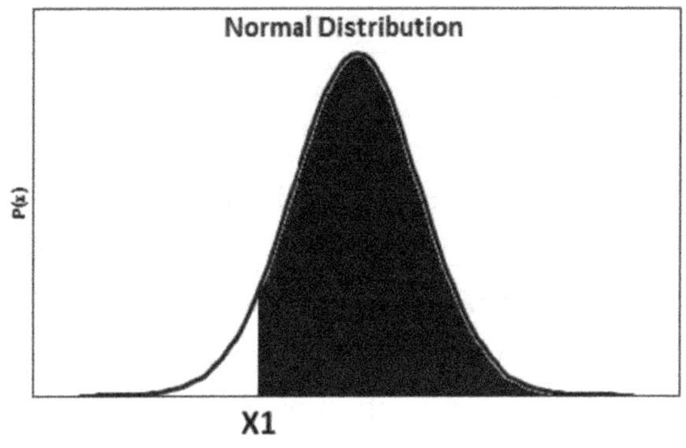

FIGURE 28 Case C: Keyword—Between X1 and X2

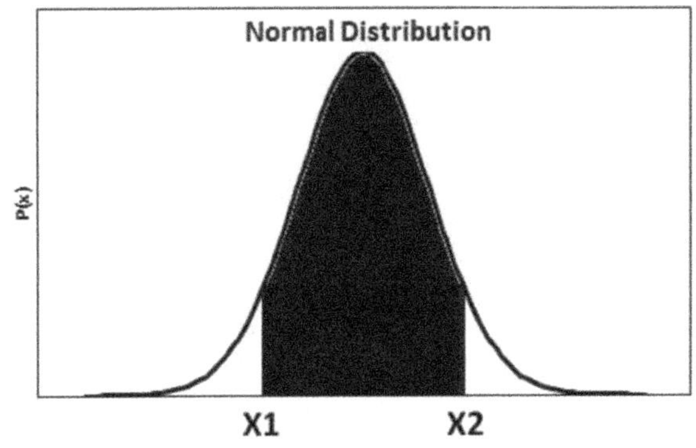

FIGURE 29 Case D: Keyword—Less Than X1 or Greater Than X2

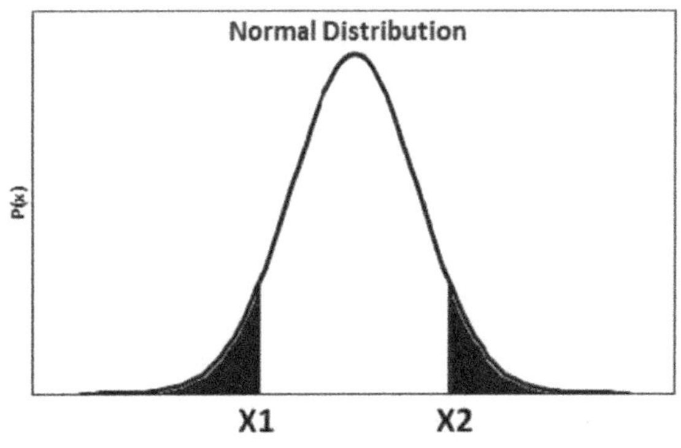

TABLE 12 Normal Distribution Formulas (Population Standard Deviation Known)

Normal Distribution Formulas (Population Standard Deviation Known)		
Convert to Z Distribution	Case—All	$Z_{\bar{X}1} = \dfrac{\bar{X}1 - \mu}{\frac{\sigma}{\sqrt{n}}}$ $Z_{\bar{X}2} = \dfrac{\bar{X}2 - \mu}{\frac{\sigma}{\sqrt{n}}}$
Result	**Case—Keyword**	**Excel Formula**
Probability $P(\bar{X} < \bar{X}1)$	Case A: Less than	=NORM.S.DIST($Z_{\bar{X}1}$,TRUE)
Probability $P(\bar{X} > \bar{X}1)$	Case B: Greater than	=1-NORM.S.DIST($Z_{\bar{X}1}$,TRUE)
Probability $P(\bar{X}1 < \bar{X} < \bar{X}2)$	Case C: Between	=NORM.S.DIST($Z_{\bar{X}2}$,TRUE)-NORM.S.DIST($Z_{\bar{X}1}$,TRUE)
Probability $P(\bar{X} < \bar{X}1$ or $\bar{X} > \bar{X}2)$	Case D: Less than OR Greater than	=1-NORM.S.DIST($Z_{\bar{X}2}$,TRUE)+ NORM.S.DIST($Z_{\bar{X}1}$,TRUE)
Mean	All	μ
Standard Deviation	All	σ
Standard Error	All	$SE = \frac{\sigma}{\sqrt{n}}$

Where:

- $\bar{X}$ is the random variable
- $Z_{\bar{X}_1}$ is the value of $\bar{X}1$ when converted to the standard normal distribution
- $Z_{\bar{X}_2}$ is the value of $\bar{X}2$ when converted to the standard normal distribution
- $\bar{X}1$ and $\bar{X}2$ are the limits of the probability areas
- μ is the population mean
- σ is the population standard deviation
- SE is the Standard Error

TABLE 13 Normal Distribution Formulas (Population Standard Deviation Unknown)

Normal Distribution Formulas (Population Standard Deviation Unknown)		
Convert to T Distribution	Case—All	$T_{\bar{X}1} = \frac{\bar{X}1 - \mu}{\frac{s}{\sqrt{n}}}$ $T_{\bar{X}2} = \frac{\bar{X}2 - \mu}{\frac{s}{\sqrt{n}}}$ dof $= n - 1$
Result	**Case—Keyword**	**Excel Formula**
Probability $P(\bar{X} < \bar{X}1)$	Case A: Less than	=T.DIST($T_{\bar{X}1}$,dof,TRUE)
Probability $P(\bar{X} > v1)$	Case B: Greater than	=1-T.DIST($T_{\bar{X}1}$,dof,TRUE)
Probability $P(\bar{X}1 < \bar{X} < \bar{X}2)$	Case C: Between	=T.DIST($T_{\bar{X}2}$,dof,TRUE)-T.DIST($T_{\bar{X}1}$,dof,TRUE)
Probability $P(\bar{X} < \bar{X}1$ or $\bar{X} > \bar{X}2)$	Case D: Less than OR Greater than	=1-T.DIST($T_{\bar{X}2}$,dof,TRUE)+ T.DIST($T_{\bar{X}1}$,dof,TRUE)
Mean	All	μ
Standard Deviation	All	σ
Standard Error	All	$SE = \frac{s}{\sqrt{n}}$

Where:

- $\bar{X}$ is the random variable
- $T_{\bar{X}_1}$ is the value of $\bar{X}1$ when converted to the T distribution
- $T_{\bar{X}_2}$ is the value of $\bar{X}2$ when converted to the T distribution
- $\bar{X}1$ and $\bar{X}2$ are the limits of the probability areas
- μ is the population mean
- σ and σ^2 (population standard deviation and variance) are unknown
- s is the sample standard deviation
- n is the sample size
- SE is the Standard Error

Normal Probability Distribution Example Problem

AutoLight manufactures headlight bulbs for automobiles. The CEO claims that an average AutoLight bulb lasts 650 days. A researcher randomly selects 40 bulbs for testing and the sample standard deviation is 50 days.

a. Identify the correct type of probability distribution for this case
b. Find the probability that the population mean is actually < 630 days
c. Find the probability that the population mean is actually > 630 days
d. Find the probability that the population mean is actually between 630 and 670 days
e. Find the probability that the population mean is actually < 620 or > 650 days

TABLE 14 Normal Probability Distribution Solution Example

	A	B	C	D
1	**Information Given in Problem**			
2	Population Mean (CEO Claim)	μ	650	
3	Population Standard Deviation	σ	Unknown	
4	Sample Size	n	40	
5	Sample Standard Deviation	s	50	
6	Degrees of Freedom	dof	39	
7				
8	**a. Decision Tree**			
9	Is the probability distribution continuous	Yes		
10	Are the probabilities equal	No		
11	Is the distribution described by the rate	No		
12	Is the random variable a sample mean	Yes		
13	Normal, since Population σ Unknown t distribution			
14				
15		**Probability Boundaries**	**Tstat**	**Formula**
16	$\bar{X}1$	630	-2.53	=(B16-$D$2) /($D$5/SQRT($D$4))
17	$\bar{X}2$	670	2.53	=(B17-$D$2) /($D$5/SQRT($D$4))
18				

19	Question	Probability	Formula
20	b. Probability < 630 days	0.78%	=T.DIST(C16,D6,TRUE)
21	c. Probability > 630 days	99.22%	=1-T.DIST(C16,D6,TRUE)
22	d. Probability between 630 and 670 days	98.44%	=T.DIST(C17,D6,TRUE)-T.DIST(C16,D6,TRUE)
23	e. Probability < 630 or > 670 days	1.56%	=1-T.DIST(C17,D6,TRUE)+ T.DIST(C16,D6,TRUE)

Video Available: Watch the Chapter 4—Normal T Distribution Video

Video Available: Watch the Chapter 4—Normal Z Distribution Video

Reference

Lind, D. A. (2015). *Statistical Techniques in Business & Economics Six.* New York, NY: McGraw-Hill Education.

CHAPTER 5

INFERENTIAL STATISTICS
Hypothesis Testing

In probability and statistics, a hypothesis is a statement about a population parameter subject to statistical test. Hypothesis testing is a procedure based on sample evidence and probability theory to determine whether the hypothesis is a reasonable statement. A hypothesis test consists of two statements about the population parameter that is being tested:

- The Null Hypothesis (H_0) is a statement about the value of a population parameter developed for the purpose of testing numerical evidence.
- The Alternative Hypothesis (H_1) is a statement that is accepted if the sample data provides sufficient evidence that the null hypothesis is false.

From a practical standpoint, business professionals can use hypothesis tests in many ways. For example, companies are always looking for better ways of doing things. Thus, we might want to compare the results of various ways of doing things. In other words, we may want to compare the results of different processes. For example, we might have a process in place and we might look for ways to improve upon this existing process. If this is the case, we could use hypothesis tests to support that the new process is perhaps at least as good as the existing one, or perhaps that it is performing better than the existing process based on some sort of measurement of interest (i.e., time, cost, quality, etc.).

It should be noted that there are many forms of hypothesis tests. For example, we can make inferences about a population's mean, variance, or frequency. In this chapter, our focus will be to introduce hypothesis tests for inferences related to means.

In this chapter, we will be investigating three types of hypothesis tests, which are outlined below.

- Single Sample Hypothesis Tests
- Two-Sample Hypothesis Tests
- Multi-Sample or Multi-Factor Hypothesis Tests

In general, single sample hypothesis tests are used when you would like to make an inference about a population's mean when you have one sample of information. For example, practitioners might want to know if there has been some sort of shift, or a change, in the population's mean. Assuming that we know the population's mean and we have access to our sample data, we can conduct a hypothesis test to make inferences about whether there is sufficient evidence that would indicate that the population's mean value has changed. If we conclude that a shift has occurred, we might come to the realization that something significant is causing our process to become unstable. Another alternative interpretation could be that something about the process we are measuring has changed and perhaps the process is performing better or worse than it has been historically.

Two-sample hypothesis tests are used when you would like to make an inference about the mean values for two different populations. For these tests, we are simply wanting to determine if the means from these two populations are perhaps different, or perhaps one is less than or one is greater than the other. For example, let us assume that we are trying to evaluate two different process designs that accomplish the same task. We might want to see if there is a statistical difference between the two processes. We might be able to conclude, given the sample information that we collected, that the two processes are performing statistically equivalent to each other. If this is the case, we might want to choose the less costly option. If this is not the case, we might want to conduct an additional hypothesis test in order to determine which process is "better" from a performance perspective (i.e., time, quality, etc.).

The third category of hypothesis tests that we will explore is called the multi-sample or multi-factor hypothesis test. Up until now, we have introduced a single and two-sample hypothesis test, which have been defined by the number of samples that we use in order to make inferences about a population. Multi-sample simply means that we can conduct similar hypothesis tests when we have more than two samples. However, in order to explore multi-sample hypothesis tests, we will need to explore different statistical tests in order to make inferences about the population's mean values. Another concept related to multi-sample hypothesis testing is a concept known as a factor. If we think about three samples, we might consider naming the samples based on where or how they were obtained. For example, we might have three samples called Process 1, Process 2, and Process 3. In this case, we have a multi-sample type of problem simply because we have three samples. However, the process itself acts as a factor in our hypothesis test. Now consider the same experiment that was previously described where we have three employees conducting each process. If this is the case, we have now just introduced an additional factor into our study. Thus, our experiment would be a multi-sample and multi-factor hypothesis test. From an application standpoint, we might want to isolate the effects that employees have on each process, or similarly, we might want to isolate the effect that each process has on each employee. Regardless, we might want to make inferences to determine if a factor is statistically equivalent, or perhaps if at least one factor is different from the others.

Important Things to Remember About H_0 and H_1

- H_0 is the null hypothesis and H_1 is the alternate hypothesis
- H_0 and H_1 are mutually exclusive and collectively exhaustive
- H_0 is always presumed to be true, and H_1 has the burden of proof
- A random sample (n) is used to **reject** or **fail to reject** H_0
- Another way to say fail to reject H_0 is to say do not reject H_0

- If we do not reject H_0, it does not necessarily mean that H_0 is true. This conclusion only suggests that there is not sufficient evidence to reject H_0. Therefore, rejecting H_0 suggests that there is significant evidence that H_1 **may be** true.
- When writing hypothesis statements, remember that the equality sign is always a part of H_0 (i.e., "=", "≥", "≤") and inequalities are always a part of H_1 (i.e., "≠", "<", and ">")

Selecting the Correct Type of Hypothesis Test

- Use the Decision Tree for Hypothesis Testing shown in Figure 1 to select the correct type of hypothesis test to use

Type I (Alpha) and Type II (Beta) Error

There are two types of errors associated with hypothesis tests. A researcher can reject H_0 when it is actually true (i.e., Type I Error) and a researcher can fail to reject the null hypothesis when it is actually false (i.e., Type II Error).

- Type I Error
  * is defined as the probability of rejecting the H_0 when it is actually true
  * is denoted by the Greek letter alpha (i.e., α)
  * α is also known as the significance level of a test
- Type II Error
  * is defined as the probability of failing to reject the null hypothesis when it is actually false
  * is denoted by the Greek letter beta (i.e., β)
  * 1- β is considered the power of the hypothesis test
  * The power is the probability of rejecting the null hypothesis when it is false

TABLE 1 Hypothesis Test Error Types

Null Hypothesis Is Actually	Researcher Did Not Reject H_0	Researcher Rejected H_0
True	Correct Decision	Type I Error (α)
False	Type II Error (β)	Correct Decision

Basic Definitions II

- The **Test Statistic** is a value, determined from sample information, used to determine whether to reject or to fail to reject the null hypothesis.
- The **Critical Value** is the dividing point between the region where the null hypothesis is rejected and the region where it is not rejected.

Setting Up a Hypothesis Test

- In practice, H_0 represents status quo or what has historically been true in the past.
- We often collect new sample information because we are interested in whether there has been a change in the population's value.
- In practice, we often conduct hypothesis because we want to reject the H_0.
- Remember, H_1 has the burden of proof.
- When writing hypothesis statements, it is useful to identify keywords in the problem and convert them into symbols.
- When writing a hypothesis statement, use the keyword to write the H_1 first.

TABLE 2 Hypothesis Test Keywords

Keywords	Common Inequality Symbol	Part of
Larger than	$>$	H_1
More than	$>$	H_1
Has increased	$>$	H_1
The same	$\neq$	H_1
No change	$\neq$	H_1
Is there a difference	$\neq$	H_1
Smaller than	$<$	H_1
Less than	$<$	H_1
Has decreased	$<$	H_1

It should be noted that the context of the problem should be taken into account when writing hypothesis statements. At times there might be a logical confusion based on some forms of measurements. For example, for most measurements that we take, larger values are often better values. However, this is not always the case in practice. Consider time measurements. In the context of better, better is not associated with a larger number but rather smaller ones. Thus, when writing hypothesis statements critically evaluate the measurement of the value of interest and pair that correctly with the correct logical operator.

FIGURE 1 Decision Tree for Hypothesis Testing

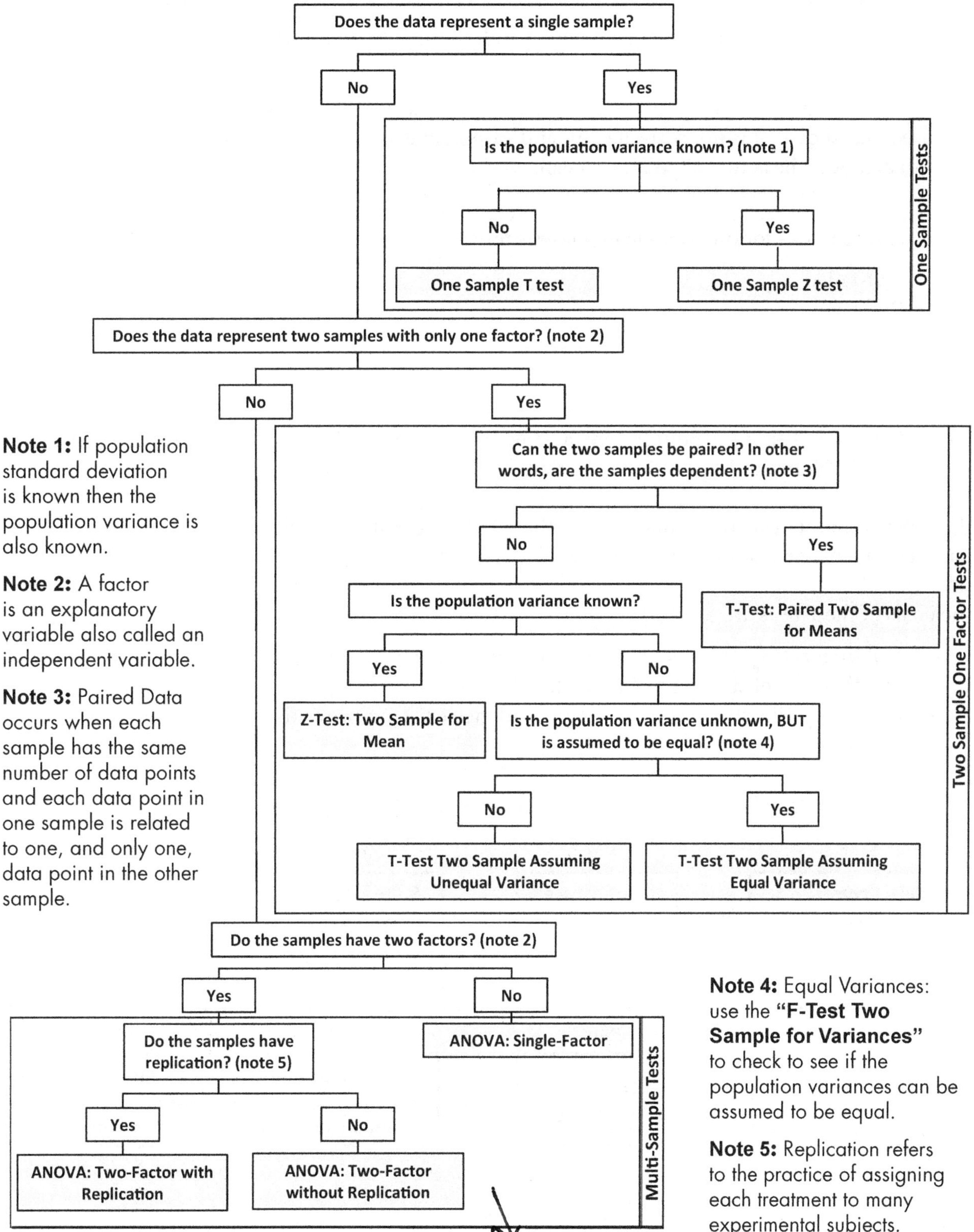

Note 1: If population standard deviation is known then the population variance is also known.

Note 2: A factor is an explanatory variable also called an independent variable.

Note 3: Paired Data occurs when each sample has the same number of data points and each data point in one sample is related to one, and only one, data point in the other sample.

Note 4: Equal Variances: use the **"F-Test Two Sample for Variances"** to check to see if the population variances can be assumed to be equal.

Note 5: Replication refers to the practice of assigning each treatment to many experimental subjects.

Always a right tailed test

One-Sample Hypothesis Tests

(Comparing the results of a single sample to a population value)

Based on sample data, we are testing to see whether or not the actual population mean is different from the given or stated population mean. Sample data is used to test for actual population means because in most cases it is not cost-effective and/or possible to collect data on the entire population in order to compute the actual population mean.

There are three cases for one-sample hypothesis tests:

- Left-tailed
- Right-tailed
- Two-tailed

In addition, there are two types of tests:

- Use the **Z-Test** if the **population variance** and/or standard deviation is **known** or given
- Use the **T-Test** if the **population variance** and/or standard deviation is **unknown** or not given

The most common level of significance for these tests is $\alpha = 0.05$ which is 5%. If α is not given, it is common practice to assume that α is 0.05.

The goals of these tests are to either:

- **Fail to reject H_0**: This does not necessarily mean that the null hypothesis is true, it only suggests that there is not sufficient evidence to reject H_0;
- **Reject H_0**: This suggests that enough evidence exists to prove that the alternative hypothesis is true

FIGURE 2 Stepwise Procedure for Single-Sample Hypothesis Tests

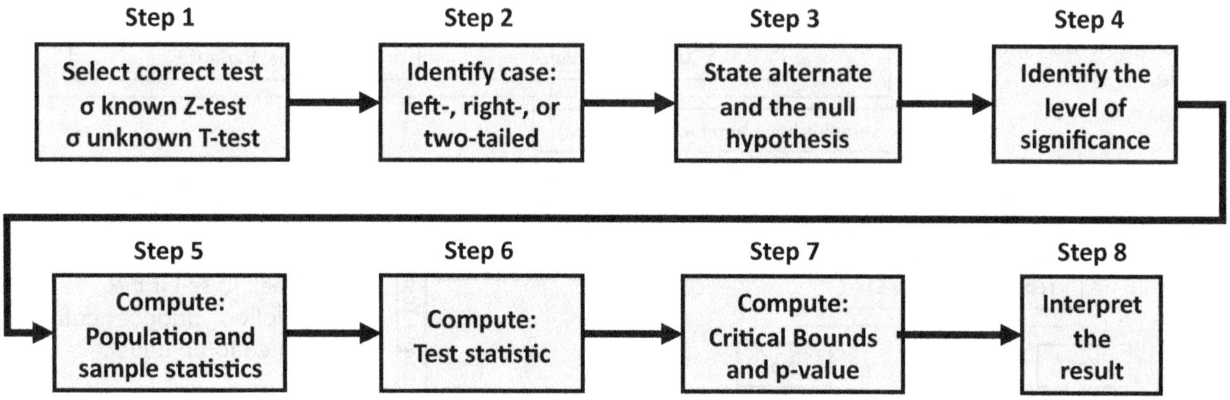

Cases and Hypothesis

FIGURE 3 Left-, Right-, and Two-Tailed Cases and Hypothesis

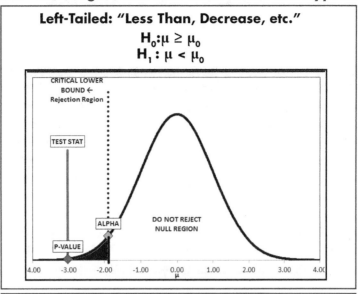

Left-Tailed: "Less Than, Decrease, etc."

$$H_0: \mu \geq \mu_0$$
$$H_1: \mu < \mu_0$$

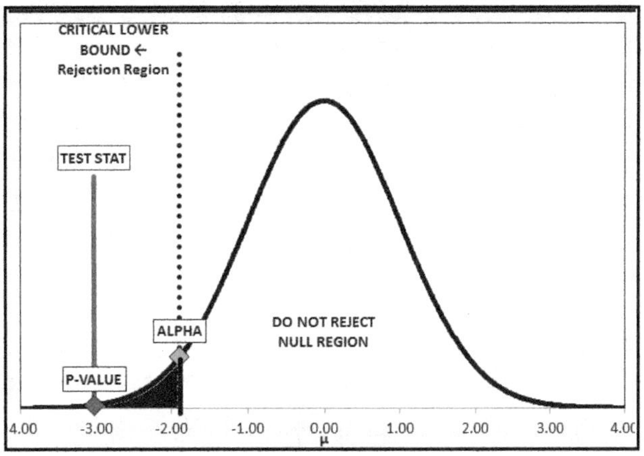

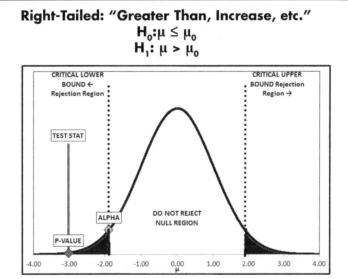

Right-Tailed: "Greater Than, Increase, etc."

$$H_0: \mu \leq \mu_0$$
$$H_1: \mu > \mu_0$$

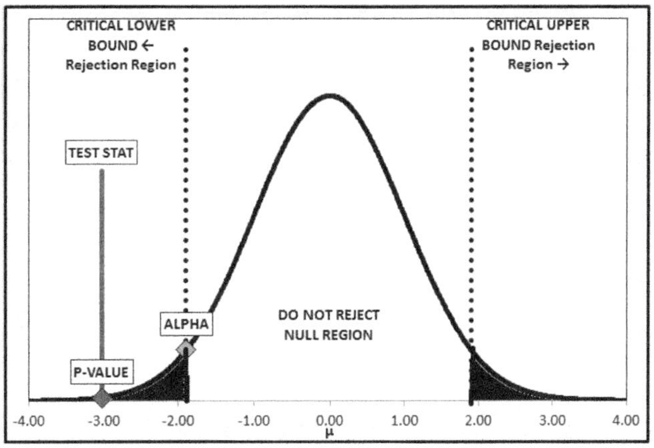

Two-Tailed: "Difference, Change, etc."

$$H_0: \mu = \mu_0$$
$$H_1: \mu \neq \mu_0$$

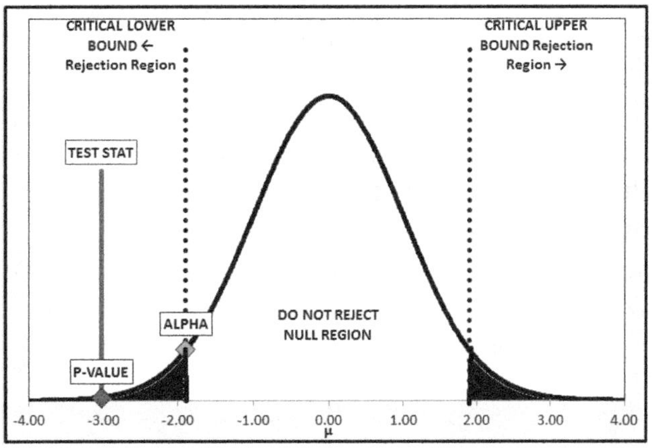

TABLE 3 Excel Formulas for One-Sample Hypothesis Testing

Population Standard Deviation Known: Use Z Test				
Test Statistic: $Z_{stat} = \frac{\bar{X} - \mu}{\frac{\sigma}{\sqrt{n}}}$				
Test Direction	**Z_{crit} Lower Bound**	**Z_{crit} Upper Bound**	**p-value**	**Reject H_0 if**
Two-Tailed	=NORM.S.INV(α/2)	=NORM.S.INV(1-α/2)	=2*NORM.S.DIST (-1*ABS(Z_{stat}),TRUE)	$\|Z_{stat}\| > Z_{crit}$
Left-Tailed	=NORM.S.INV(α)	N/A	=NORM.S.DIST (-1*ABS(Z_{stat}),TRUE)	$Z_{stat} < Z_{crit}$
Right-Tailed	N/A	=NORM.S.INV(1-α)	=NORM.S.DIST (-1*ABS(Z_{stat}),TRUE)	$Z_{stat} > Z_{crit}$

Population Standard Deviation Unknown: Use T-Test				
Test Statistic: $T_{stat} = \frac{\bar{X} - \mu}{\frac{s}{\sqrt{n}}}$				
Test Direction	**T_{crit} Lower Bound**	**T_{crit} Upper Bound**	**p-value**	**Reject H_0 if**
Two-Tailed	=(-1)*T.INV.2T(α,dof)	=T.INV.2T(α,dof)	=T.DIST.2T(ABS(T_{stat}),dof)	$\|T_{stat}\| > \|T_{crit}\|$
Left-Tailed	=T.INV(α,dof)	N/A	=T.DIST (-1*ABS(T_{stat}),dof,TRUE)	$T_{stat} < T_{crit}$
Right-Tailed	N/A	=T.INV(1-α,dof)	=T.DIST (-1*ABS(T_{stat}),dof,TRUE)	$T_{stat} > T_{crit}$

All Tests: Reject H_0 if p-value < alpha

NOTE: |number| indicates Absolute Value, which in Excel is ABS(number)

Where:

- α is alpha and is the level of significance (usually 0.01, 0.05, or 0.10)
- H_0 is the null hypothesis and H_1 is the alternate hypothesis
- μ_0 is the historical or existing population mean (Mu)
- μ is the "new" population mean that you are attempting to prove
- $\bar{X}$ is the sample mean that you use to prove the "new" mean, use AVERAGE function to calculate from data
- Z_{stat} and T_{stat} are the test statistics used to determine whether to reject the null hypothesis
- Z_{crit} and T_{crit} are the dividing points between the region where the null hypothesis is rejected and the region where it is not rejected
- σ is the population standard deviation
- s is the sample standard deviation if given sample data use STDEV.S function to calculate
- n is the sample size
- dof = n-1 (degrees of freedom)

Single-Sample Problem and Solution Example

The Ohio EPA reports that the per capita water use in a single family home is 72 gallons per day with a standard deviation of 10 gallons. The City of Athens recently randomly sampled 40 homes within the city and the sample mean for these homes was 67 gallons per day. At the 0.05 level of significance, is this survey enough evidence to conclude that residents of Athens use less water than the average resident of Ohio?

TABLE 4 Single-Sample Problem Solution

	A	B
1	**Questions and Answers**	
2	a. What is the correct test in this case?	One-sample Z test
3	b. Is it a left-, right-, or two-tailed case?	Left-tailed
4	c. What is the null hypothesis?	Athens μ water use >= Ohio μ water use
5	d. What is the alternate hypothesis?	Athens μ water use < Ohio μ water use
6	e. What is the level of significance?	5%
7	f. What is the population mean?	72
8	g. What is the population standard deviation?	10
9	h. What is the sample mean?	67
10	i. What is the sample size?	40
11	j. What is the value of the test statistic?	-3.16
12	k. What is the value of the critical lower bound?	-1.64
13	l. What is the value of the critical upper bound?	N/A
14	m. What is the value of the p-value?	0.08%
15	n. Should the null hypothesis be accepted or rejected?	Reject H_0
16–17	o. State the result in plain English	The average Athens water use is less than the overall average Ohio water use
18		
19	**Formulas**	
20	Test Statistic Formula from cell B11	=(B9-B7)/(B8/SQRT(B10))
21	Critical Lower Bound Formula from cell B12	=NORM.S.INV(B6)
22	p-value Formula from cell B14	=NORM.S.DIST(-1*ABS(B11),TRUE)

FIGURE 4 Visualization of Water Usage Hypothesis Test Solution

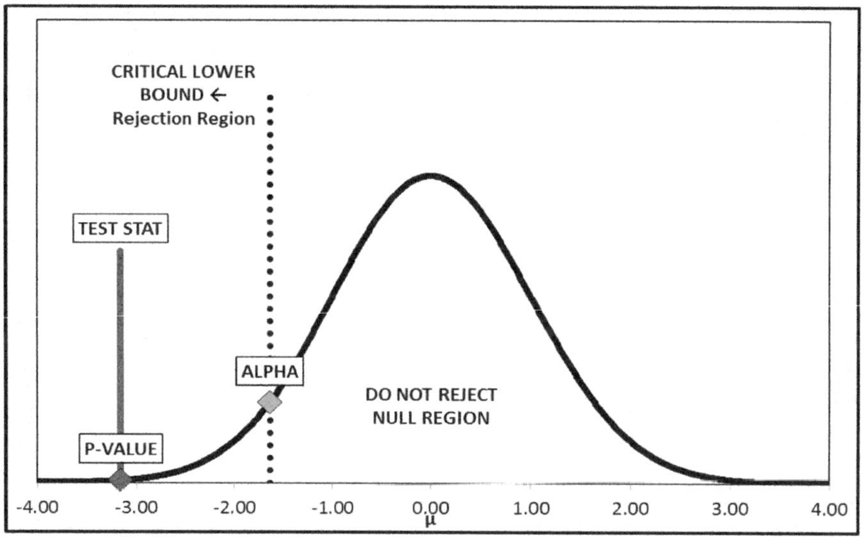

Video Available: Watch the Chapter 5—One Sample Z Test—Left-Tailed Video

Video Available: Watch the Chapter 5—One Sample T Test—Right-Tailed Video

Video Available: Watch the Chapter 5—One Sample T Test—Two-Tailed Video

Two-Sample, One Factor Hypothesis Tests for Means

(Comparing the results of two samples to their population values)

Based on sample data, we are testing to see whether the means in two populations are the same or different. Sample data is used to test for actual population means because in most cases it is not cost-effective and/or possible to collect data on the entire population in order to compute the actual population mean.

There are three cases for two-sample tests:

- Left-tailed
- Right-tailed
- Two-tailed

In addition, there are four types of tests:

- Use the **"T-Test: Paired Two-Sample for Means"** if the **samples are paired,** paired data are samples with the same number of data points and each point in one sample is related to one, and only one, data point in the other sample.

- Use the **"Z-Test: Two-Sample for Means"** if the samples are **not paired** and the **population variance is known.**
- Use the **"T-Test: Two-Sample Assuming Unequal Variance"** if the samples are **not paired,** the **population variance is unknown** and **cannot be assumed to be equal.**
- Use the **"T-Test: Two-Sample Assuming Equal Variance"** if the samples are **not paired**, the **population variance is unknown** but **can be assumed to be equal.**

The most common level of significance for these tests is α = 0.05 which is 5%. If α is not given, it is common practice to assume that α is 0.05. The goals of these tests are to either:

- **Fail to reject H_0**: This does not necessarily mean that the null hypothesis is true, it only suggests that there is not sufficient evidence to reject H_0;
- **Reject H_0**: This suggests that enough evidence exists to prove that the alternative hypothesis is true.

FIGURE 5 Stepwise Procedure for Two-Sample Hypothesis Tests

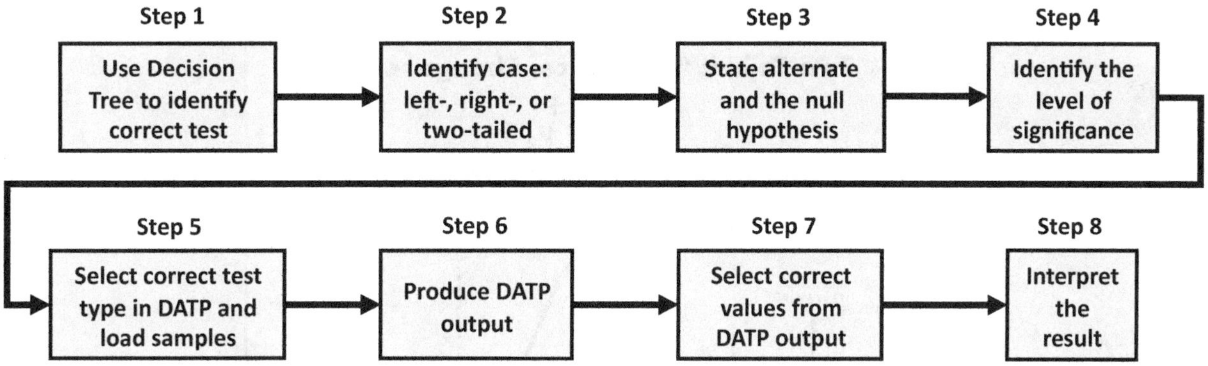

Cases and Hypothesis

FIGURE 6 Left-, Right-, and Two-Tailed Cases and Hypothesis

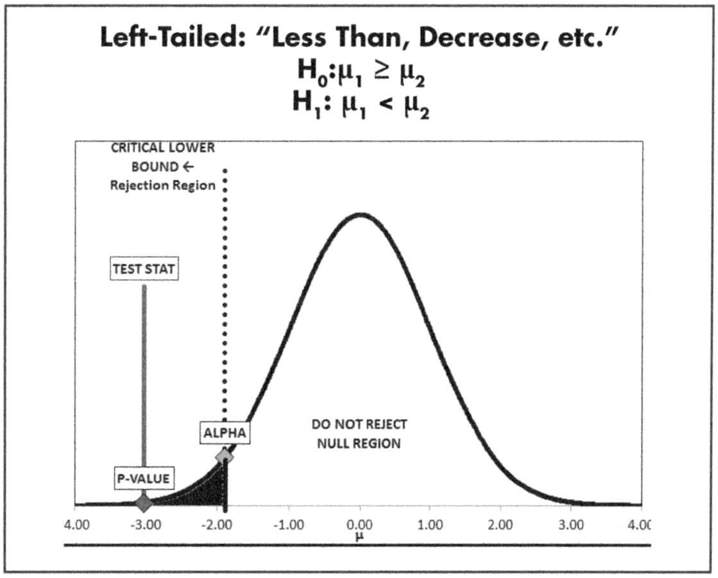

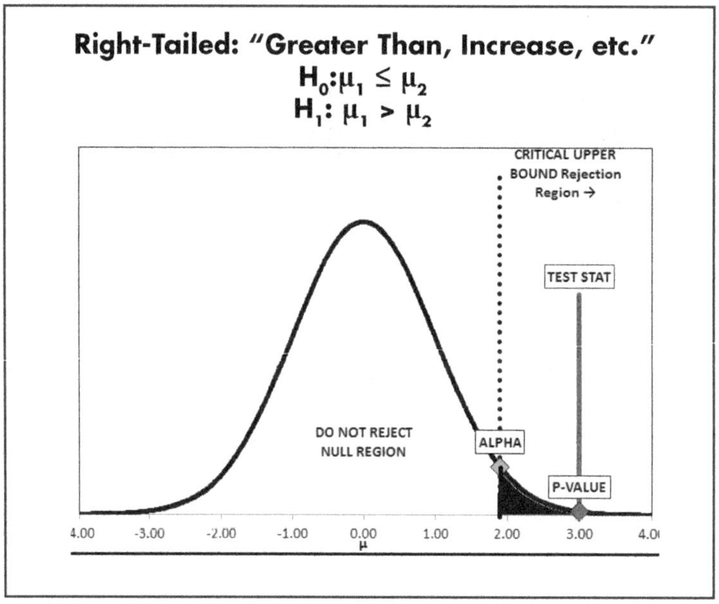

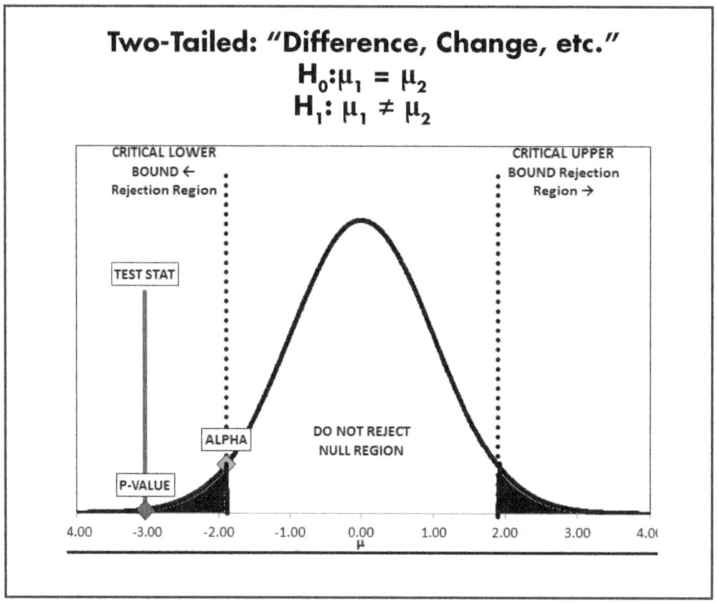

Excel DATP Input Fields

- DATP Test names match the decision tree test names
- Variable 1 Range: first sample data
- Variable 2 Range: second sample data
- Hypothesized Mean Difference: usually this is zero (blank)
- Labels: recommend using labels
- Alpha: level of significance
- Output Range: the first cell on spreadsheet to place output data

Interpreting the results—Reject H_0 if:

- Two-Tailed: |t-stat| > t Critical two-tail
- Left-Tailed: t-stat< -t Critical one-tail
- Right-Tailed: t-stat > t Critical one-tail
- All Tests: p-value < alpha

Where:

- α is alpha and is the level of significance (usually .01, .05, or .10)
- H_0 is the null hypothesis and H_1 is the alternate hypothesis
- μ_1 is the first population mean
- μ_2 is the second population mean
- Parameters output from Excel Data Analysis ToolPak (DATP)
  * Mean: sample means from two samples
  * Variance: sample variance from two samples
  * df: degrees of freedom
  * t-stat: the test statistic (will be output as positive or negative depending on variable range 1 and 2 selection)
  * P(T<=t) one-tail: p-value for left- or right-tailed tests
  * t Critical one-tail: critical upper bound is output, critical lower bound is negative of the output value
  * P(T<=t) two-tail: p-value for two-tailed tests
  * t Critical two-tail: critical upper bound is output, critical lower bound is negative of the output value

Two-Sample Problem and Solution Example

A corporate manager of a major furniture outlet recently wanted to see if there was a difference in the dollar value of sales between the men and women he employs as sales associates. To research his hypothesis, he selected a couple random samples of sales data out of his sales database. The random sample in column A shows the daily sales of 40 men at random locations. The random sample in column B shows the daily sales of 50 women at random locations. Assume the population standard deviation for men is \$210 and for women is \$245. At a significance level of .05 significance, can the manager conclude that the mean amount sold per day is larger for the women?

TABLE 5 Two-Sample Problem Solution

	A	B	C	D	E
1	**Men**	**Women**	**Solution**		
2	$1,646	$1,829	Step 1: Select correct test	Two-sample with σ given	Z-Test: Two-Sample for Means
3	$1,528	$1,783	Step 2: Identify the Random Samples	Column A: Men's sales	Column B: Women's sales
4	$1,625	$1,720	Step 3: State alternate and null hypothesis	Null: Women's sales <= men's sales	Alternate: women's sales > men's sales
5	$1,506	$1,773	Step 4: Identify level of significance	alpha given	5%
6	$1,690	$1,631	Step 5: Select correct test type in DATP and load samples	Men population standard deviation σ	210
7	$1,518	$1,637		Women population standard deviation σ	245
8	$1,663	$1,659		Men population variance	44100
9	$1,549	$1,825		Women population variance	60025
10	$1,536	$1,681	Step 6: Produce DATP Output		
11	$1,602	$1,737			
12	$1,586	$1,686	Step 7: Select correct values from DATP output	Zstat	2.14
13	$1,578	$1,816		Zcrit upper bound	1.64
14	$1,591	$1,634		p-value	1.63%
15	$1,604	$1,809	Step 8: Interpret the result	Reject H_0 if Zstat > Zcrit	Reject H_0
16	$1,678	$1,780		Reject H_0 if pvalue < alpha	Reject H_0
17	$1,627	$1,644			
18	$1,553	$1,640	**Data Analysis Tool Pak Output**		
19	$1,636	$1,644	z-Test: Two-Sample for Means		
20	$1,585	$1,665		Women	Men
21	$1,663	$1,680	Mean	1728.96	1598.714286
22	$1,565	$1,708	Known Variance	60025.00	44100
23	$1,512	$1,857	Observations	28.00	28
24	$1,648	$1,869	Hypothesized Mean Difference	0.00	
25	$1,594	$1,644	z	2.14	
26	$1,696	$1,680	P(Z<=z) one-tail	1.63%	
27	$1,584	$1,821	z Critical one-tail	1.64	
28	$1,685	$1,765	P(Z<=z) two-tail	0.03	
29	$1,516	$1,794	z Critical two-tail	1.96	

Video Available: Watch the Chapter 5—Z-Test: Two-Sample for Means Video

Video Available: Watch the Chapter 5—T-Test: Paired Two-Sample for Means Video

Video Available: Watch the Chapter 5—T-Test: Two-Sample Assuming Unequal Variance Video

Video Available: Watch the Chapter 5—T-Test: Two-Sample Assuming Equal Variance Video

Multi-Sample or Multi-Factor Hypothesis Tests—for Means

(Comparing the results of more than two samples to their population values)

Comparing Means of Two or More Populations With ANOVA

- ANOVA (Analysis of Variance) to test the equality of more than two population means
- Assumes populations follow the normal distribution
- Assumes populations have equal variances
- Assumes populations are independent
- The Null Hypothesis is that the population means are all the same
- The Alternative Hypothesis is that at least one of the means is different
- The Test Statistic is the F distribution
- The Decision rule is to reject the null hypothesis if F is greater than F_{crit}
- Factor: an explanatory variable also called an independent variable
- Replication: refers to the practice of assigning each treatment to many experimental subjects

FIGURE 7 Stepwise Procedure for Multi-Sample Hypothesis Tests

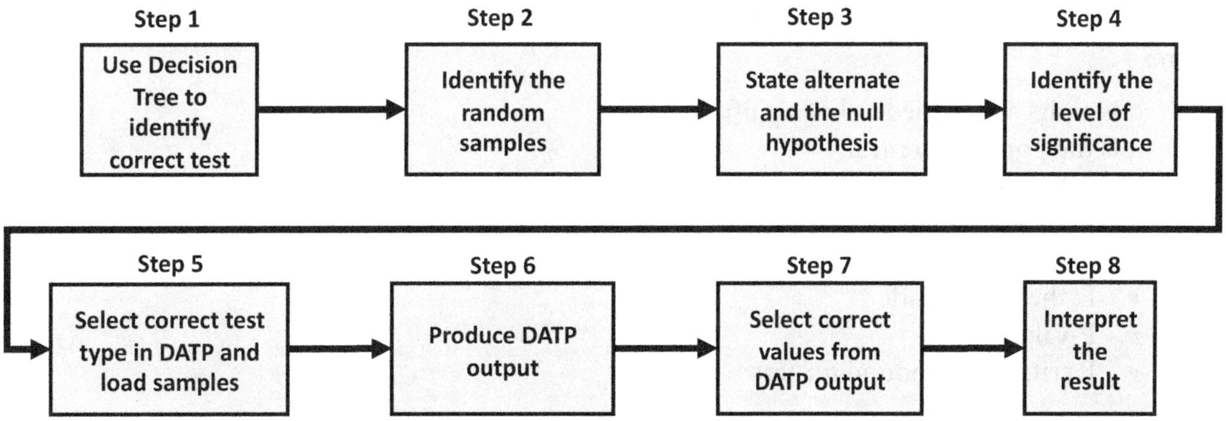
Step 1
Use Decision Tree to identify correct test
Step 2
Identify the random samples
Step 3
State alternate and the null hypothesis
Step 4
Identify the level of significance
Step 5
Select correct test type in DATP and load samples
Step 6
Produce DATP output
Step 7
Select correct values from DATP output
Step 8
Interpret the result

FIGURE 8 F Distribution for Multi-Sample Hypothesis Tests

H_0: all means are equal
H_1: all means are not equal

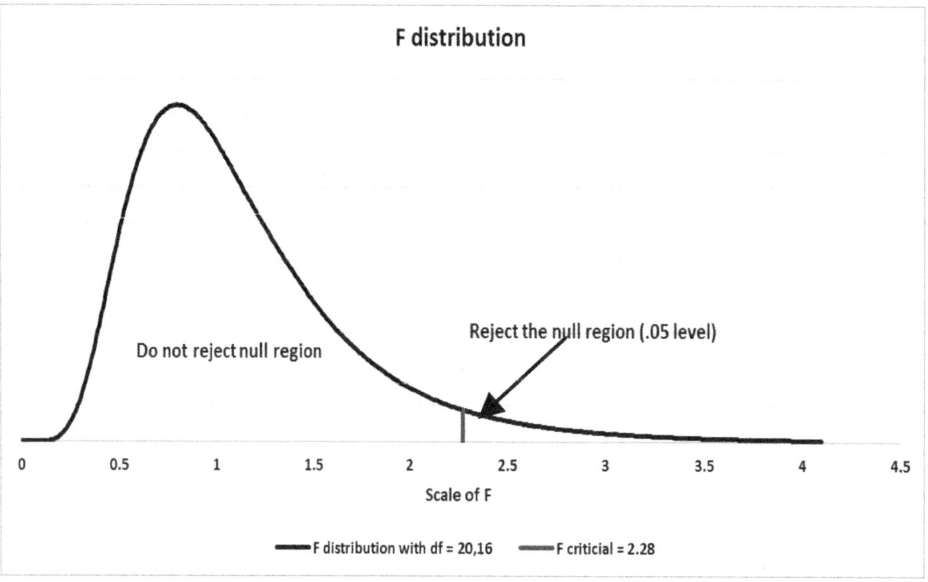

Excel DATP Input Fields

- DATP Test names match the decision tree test names
- Input Range: all sample values along with headers
- Labels: recommend using labels
- Alpha: level of significance
- Output Range: the first cell on spreadsheet to place output data

Interpreting the results: Reject H_0 if

- F > F crit (separate test for each factor)
- P-value < Alpha (separate test for each factor)

Where:

- α is alpha and is the level of significance
- μ is the population mean
- H_0 is the null hypothesis
- H_1 is the alternate hypothesis
- Parameters output from DATP
  - F: the test statistic
  - P-value
  - F crit: critical bound for test

Multi-Sample Problem and Solution Example

John Smith is a frequent traveler between Columbus, Ohio, and Washington, DC. For the past month, he wrote down the flight times on three different airlines. The results are shown in the table to the left.

a. Use the 0.05 significance level to check if there is a difference in the mean flight times among the three airlines.

TABLE 6 Multi-Sample Problem Solution

	A	B	C	D	E	F
1	**Skyway**	**Jetset**	**Newway**	**Solution**		
2	51	50	52	Step 1: Select correct test	More than two samples—one factor	ANOVA: Single Factor
3	51	53	55	Step 2: Identify the Random Samples	Flight Times: Skyway, Jetset, Newway	
4	52	52	60	Step 3: State the alternative and the null hypothesis	Null: all means are equal	Alternate: all means are not equal
5	42	62	64	Step 4: Identify level of significance	alpha given	5%
6	51	53	61	Step 5: Select correct test type in DATP and load samples	See data to left for samples	
7	57	49	49	Step 6: Produce DATP Output	See below for output	
8	47	50	49	Step 7: Select correct values from DATP output	Fstat	3.20
9	47	49			Fcrit	3.27
10	50	58			p-value	5.29%
11	60	54		Step 8: Interpret the result	Reject H_0 if Fstat > Fcrit	Do not Reject H_0
12	54	51			Reject H_0 if p-value < alpha	Do not Reject H_0
13	49	49		We cannot conclude that there is a difference in the mean flight times among the three airlines		
14	48	49				
15	48	50				
16	46					
17	52					
18	55					

19	**Data Analysis ToolPak Output**					
20	Anova: Single Factor					
21						
22	SUMMARY					
23	Groups	Count	Sum	Average	Variance	
24	Skyway	17	860	50.59	18.9	
25	Jetset	14	729	52.07	14.7	
26	Newway	7	390	55.71	36.6	
27						
28						
29	ANOVA					
30	Source of Variation	SS	df	MS	F	P-value F crit
31	Between Groups	130.2884	2	65.14	3.2	0.0529 3.27
32	Within Groups	712.4748	35	20.36		
33						
34	Total	842.7632	37			

Video Available: Watch the Chapter 5—ANOVA: Single-Factor Video

Video Available: Watch the Chapter 5—ANOVA: Two-Factor without Replication Video

Two-Sample Hypothesis Tests for Equal Variances

(Comparing the results of two samples to test whether their populations have equal variances)

The F distribution is used to test the hypothesis that the variance of one normal population equals the variance of another normal population

Characteristics of F Distribution

- There is a "family" of F Distributions. A particular member of the family is determined by two parameters: the degrees of freedom in the numerator and the degrees of freedom in the denominator.
- The F distribution is continuous.
- F value cannot be negative.
- The F distribution is positively skewed.
- It is asymptotic. As F —> ∞ the curve approaches the X-axis but never touches it.
- The DATP calculates the test statistic; however, if needed the formula is $F = s_1^2/s_2^2$

FIGURE 9 Stepwise Procedure for Two-Sample Hypothesis Tests for Equal Variances

H_0: $\sigma_1^2 = \sigma_2^2$
H_1: $\sigma_1^2 \neq \sigma_2^2$

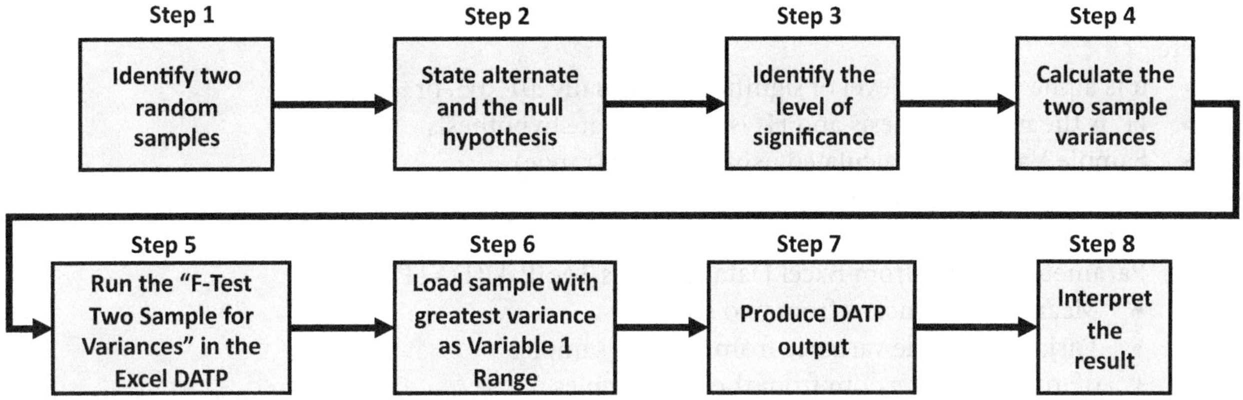
Step 1
Identify two random samples
Step 2
State alternate and the null hypothesis
Step 3
Identify the level of significance
Step 4
Calculate the two sample variances
Step 5
Run the "F-Test Two Sample for Variances" in the Excel DATP
Step 6
Load sample with greatest variance as Variable 1 Range
Step 7
Produce DATP output
Step 8
Interpret the result

Figure 10: F Distribution for Two-Sample Hypothesis Tests for Equal Variances

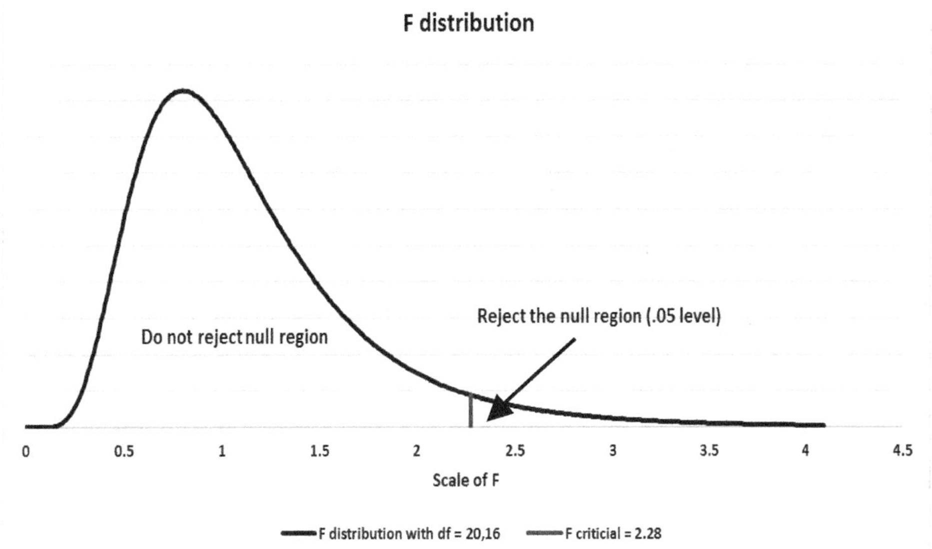
F distribution
Do not reject null region
Reject the null region (.05 level)
0
0.5
1
1.5
2
2.5
3
3.5
4
4.5
Scale of F
F distribution with df = 20,16
F criticial = 2.28

Excel DATP Input Fields

- DATP Test name is "F-Test Two-Sample for Variances"
- Variable 1 Range: sample with greater variance
- Variable 2 Range: sample with lower variance
- Labels: recommend using labels
- Alpha: level of significance
- Output Range: the first cell on spreadsheet to place output data

Interpreting the Results—Reject H_0 if

- F > F Critical one-tail
- P(F<f) one-tail < Alpha

Where:

- α is alpha and is the level of significance (usually .01, .05, or .10)
- H_0 is the null hypothesis and H_1 is the alternate hypothesis
- Sample Variance is calculated using =VAR.S(range)
- s^2 is the sample variance
- σ^2 is the population variance
- Parameters output from Excel Data Analysis ToolPak (DATP)
  - Mean: sample means from two samples
  - Variance: sample variance from the two samples
  - df: degrees of freedom from the two samples
  - F: the test statistic
  - P(T<=t) one-tail—p-value
  - F Critical one-tail—critical upper bound

P-Values in Hypothesis Testing

Basic Definitions

- The p-value is the probability of observing a sample value as extreme as, or more extreme than, the value observed, given that the null hypothesis is true.
- In testing a hypothesis, we can also compare the p-value to the level of significance (α).
- Decision rule using the p-value: **Reject H_0 if p-value < alpha.**
- If the p-value is less than alpha, accept Alternative Hypothesis.
- **The smaller the p-value the more confidence you have against the Null Hypothesis!!!**

What Does it Mean When p-value < alpha

a. If alpha = 0.10, we have some evidence that H_0 is NOT true.
b. If alpha = 0.05, we have strong evidence that H_0 is NOT true.
c. If alpha = 0.01, we have very strong evidence that H_0 is NOT true.
d. If alpha = 0.001, we have extremely strong evidence that H_0 is NOT true.

The Value of the p-value

- Determining the p-value not only results in a decision regarding H_0, but it gives us additional insight into the strength of the decision.
- A very small p-value, such as 1.54E-05, indicates that there is little likelihood the H_0 is true.
- On the other hand, a p-value of .2033 means that H_0 is not rejected, and there is little likelihood that it is false.
- The p-value is a probability so it makes sense to report it as a percentage.
- The most valuable aspect of the p-value is it allows you to remember one simple rule in order to correctly interpret the results of all types of hypothesis tests.

"If the p-value is low then the null must go"

This means that we can always Reject H_0 if p-value < alpha

CHAPTER 6

PREDICTIVE ANALYTICS
Regression

Predictive analytics involves creating mathematical models, or equations, from historic data in order to predict future outcomes. From a business perspective, we often want to be able to predict demand, sales, revenue, cost, profits, and various other things. This is useful because if we are able to predict the future, we are able to anticipate changes that we might need to make within our business before certain changes occur. In this chapter, we will study relationships between quantitative variables in the form of single and multiple linear regression. We will begin by learning how to perform a correlation analysis before moving on to simple regression.

Correlation Analysis

Correlation analysis measures the relationship between two items; for example, a company's marketing budget and their demand. The correlation or strength of the relationship between the two variables is called the coefficient of correlation.

- The basic hypothesis of correlation analysis: Does the data indicate that there is a relationship between two quantitative variables?
- Null Hypothesis: correlation in the populations is zero
- Alternate Hypothesis: correlation in the populations is different from zero
- Use a scatterplot to visualize your data
  - Helps you to "see" the relationship between the variables
  - Helps you to identify "bad" data points

The Coefficient of Correlation (R)

The **Coefficient of Correlation (R)** is a measure of the strength of the relationship between two variables

- It shows the direction and strength of the linear relationship between two interval or ratio-scale variables.
- It can range from -1.00 to +1.00.
- Values of -1.00 or +1.00 indicate perfect and strong correlation. Values close to 0.0 indicate weak correlation.
- Negative values indicate an inverse relationship and positive values indicate a direct relationship.
- The Independent Variable provides the basis for estimation. It is the predictor variable.
- The Dependent Variable is the variable being predicted or estimated.
- The Correlation Coefficient can be calculated in Excel using the **=CORREL(array1,array2)** function.

TABLE 1 Correlation Coefficient Scale for Interpretation

Negative Correlation					Positive Correlation			
Perfect Negative	Strong Negative	Moderate Negative	Weak Negative	No	Weak Positive	Moderate Positive	Strong Positive	Perfect Positive
-100.0%	-75.0%	-50.0%	-25.0%	0.0%	25.0%	50.0%	75.0%	100.0%

Using Scatterplots to Analyze for Correlation

The **Coefficient of Determination (R^2)** is a proportion of the total variation in the dependent variable Y that is explained, or accounted for, by the variation in the independent variable X.

- **R^2** is the Correlation Coefficient (R) squared
- **R^2** varies between 0 and 1. A value of 0 indicates zero predictive value, while a 1 indicates perfect prediction

FIGURE 1 Perfect Negative Correlation Example (R = -1.0 and Line has Negative Slope)

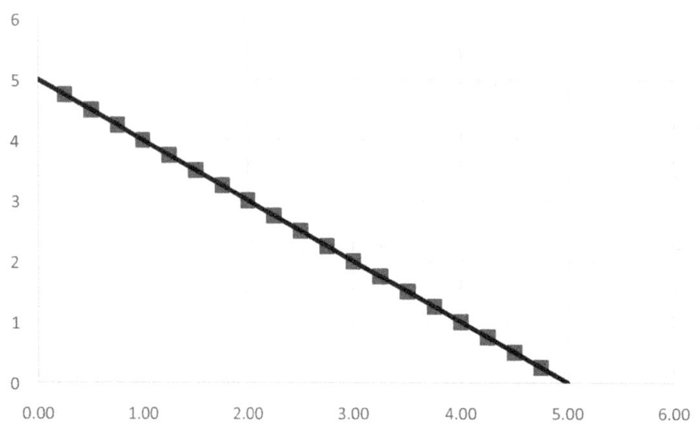

FIGURE 2 Perfect Negative Correlation Example (R = 1.0 and Line has Positive Slope)

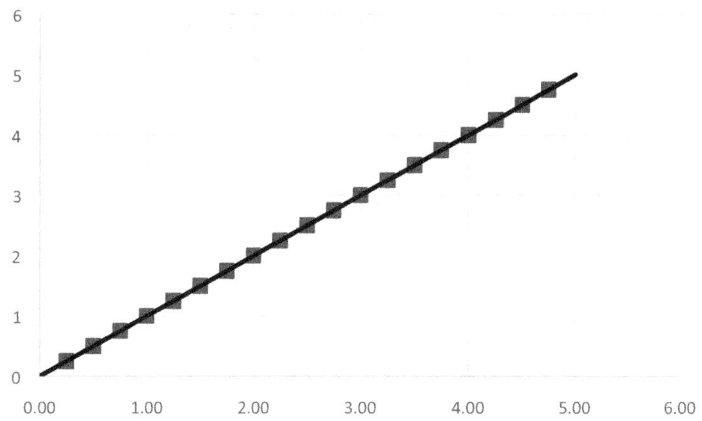

FIGURE 3 Stepwise Procedure for Testing the Significance of the Correlation Coefficient

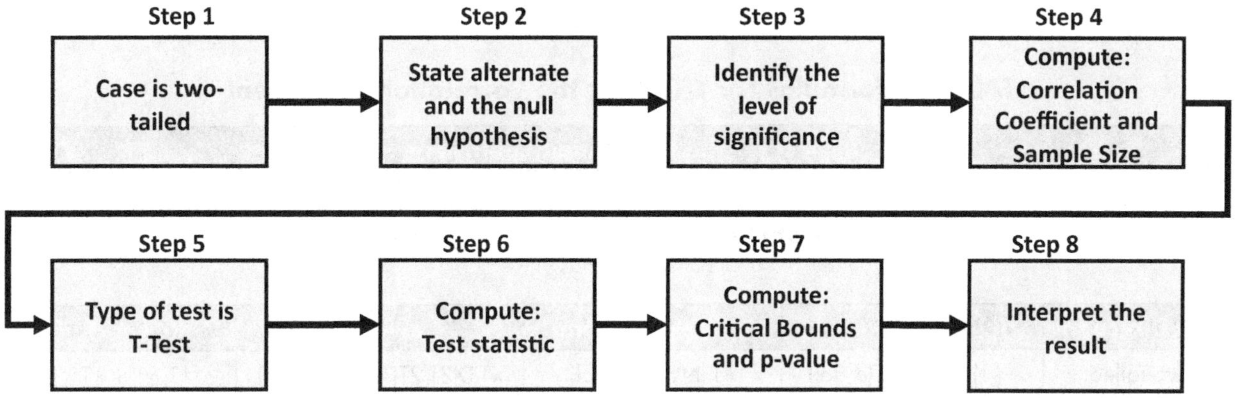

FIGURE 4 Example Correlation Coefficient Test

Two-Tailed: "Difference, Change."
H_0: correlation in the population is zero
H_1: correlation in the population is different from zero

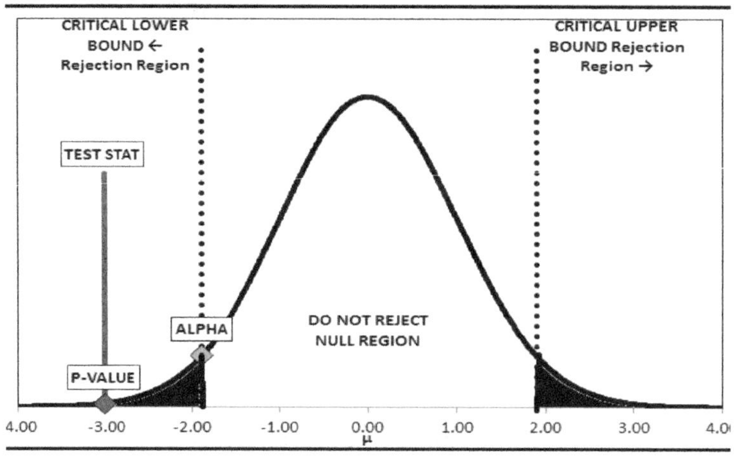

TABLE 2 Formulas for T Test for the Correlation Coefficient

T Test for the Correlation Coefficient				
Test Statistic: $T_{stat} = \frac{R\sqrt{n-2}}{\sqrt{1-R^2}}$ $dof = n-2$				
Test Direction	**T_{crit} Lower Bound**	**T_{crit} Upper Bound**	**p-value**	**Reject H_0 if**
Two-Tailed	=(-1)*T.INV.2T(α,dof)	=T.INV.2T(α,dof)	=T.DIST.2T(ABS(T_{stat}),dof)	$\lvert T_{stat}\rvert > \lvert T_{crit}\rvert$

All Tests: Reject H_0 if p-value < alpha

NOTE: |number| indicates Absolute Value, which in Excel is ABS(number)

Where:

- α is alpha and is the level of significance (usually 0.01, 0.05, or 0.10)
- H_0 is the null hypothesis and H_1 is the alternate hypothesis
- T_{stat} is the test statistic used to determine whether to reject the null hypothesis
- T_{crit} is the dividing points between the region where the null hypothesis is rejected and the region where it is not rejected
- R is the Correlation Coefficient which can be calculated in Excel using the =CORREL (array1,array2) function
- n is the sample size
- dof = n-2 (degrees of freedom)

Correlation Analysis Problem and Solution Example

A local trucking company would like to see if they could use their historical maintenance cost information to estimate future maintenance costs for their fleet of truck. Run a correlation analysis to see if the age of the truck is significantly correlated to the maintenance costs.

TABLE 3 Example Data and Solution for T-Test for the Correlation Coefficient

	A	B	C	D	E
1	**Age of Truck**	**Maintenance Cost**		**Solution**	
2	1	$1,500		Type of Test	T-Test Two-Tailed
3	2	$3,500		Null Hypothesis (H0)	Correlation is zero
4	2	$3,000		Alternate Hypothesis (H1)	Correlation is not zero
5	2	$4,000		Alpha	5%
6	3	$6,377		Correlation Coefficient (R)	0.9661
7	3	$5,305		Sample Size (n)	23
8	3	$5,797		Degrees of Freedom (dof)	21
9	3	$4,367		Test Statistic (Tstat)	17.14
10	4	$7,985		Tcrit LB	-2.08
11	4	$6,407		Tcrit UB	2.08
12	4	$6,297		pvalue	0.000000000080%
13	4	$8,717		Reject Ho if |Tstat| > |Tcrit|	Reject H_0
14	5	$10,590		Reject Ho if pvalue < alpha	Reject H_0
15	5	$9,284		We can conclude that the age of the trucks is correlated with the annual maintenance costs	
16	5	$10,135			
17	5	$11,552		Formula from Cell E6	=CORREL(A2:A24,B2:B24)
18	5	$11,999		Formula from Cell E7	=COUNT(B2:B24)
19	5	$11,596		Formula from Cell E8	=E7-2
20	6	$13,412		Formula from Cell E9	=(E6*SQRT(E7-2))/SQRT(1-E6^2)
21	6	$11,477		Formula from Cell E10	=-1*T.INV.2T(E5,E8)
22	6	$13,490		Formula from Cell E11	=T.INV.2T(E5,E8)
23	6	$12,556		Formula from Cell E12	=T.DIST.2T(ABS(E9),E8)
24	6	$14,585			

FIGURE 5 Scatterplot for Age of Truck vs. Maintenance Cost Problem

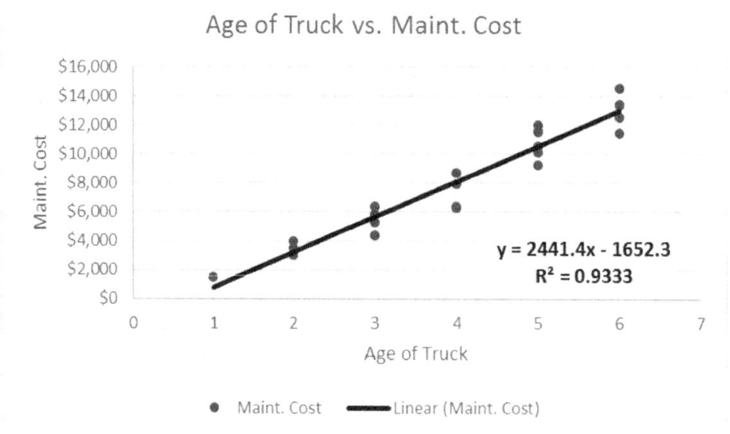

Video Available: Watch the Chapter 6—Correlation Video

Dealing With Missing Data and Outliers

Missing data and outliers in a data set can create significant problems in correlation and regression analysis; therefore it is critical to identify and properly handle these values before proceeding in your analysis. Before making any changes to your data set, save a copy of the original data in case you need to reverse any changes. Be sure to document any changes made to the original data for later reference.

Handling Missing Data

- Excel's DATP Regression tool **cannot** handle missing values in the data set
- There are several methods to treat missing values
  - Best method: Research records and insert the correct data in the missing areas
  - Next best method: Delete the record containing the missing value(s), this works best when you have a large data set compared to the number of records with missing values
  - Use the following methods with caution (these methods have negative effects on correlation and thus negative effects on the final regression model)
    - Replace missing values with mean, median, or mode of the remaining values
    - Replace missing values with a user specified value
  - Other methods (outside scope of this book)
    - Expectation Maximization
    - Multiple Imputation Methodology

Video Available: Watch the Chapter 6—Missing Values Video

Handling Outliers

- Outliers may or may not be bad data points, in general, outliers in data sets tend to lower correlation between two variables and weaken the regression model
- The process to deal with outliers is
    - First, identify possible outliers; a scatter plot is very useful in this process, plot each independent variable against the dependent variable in separate scatterplots and look for points out of place with the rest of the data.

After you identify possible outliers, find the associated record in the dataset and research it. Is the outlier a valid point? If not, correct it. If it is a valid outlier, is it a data point you want to include in your model? If not, delete the record.

Figure 6 shows an example scatterplot with an outlier for the age of truck = 1 year with associated annual maintenance costs of $14,000. Consider as an example that after researching this record, this truck was identified as being damaged in an accident. Since this was an unusual event, we may decide to remove this record before using the data to build a regression model. Note that leaving the outlier in the data significantly lowered the R^2 value from the 0.9333 shown in Figure 5 to 0.4704 in Figure 6.

FIGURE 6 Scatterplot for Age of Truck vs. Maintenance Cost Problem With an Outlier

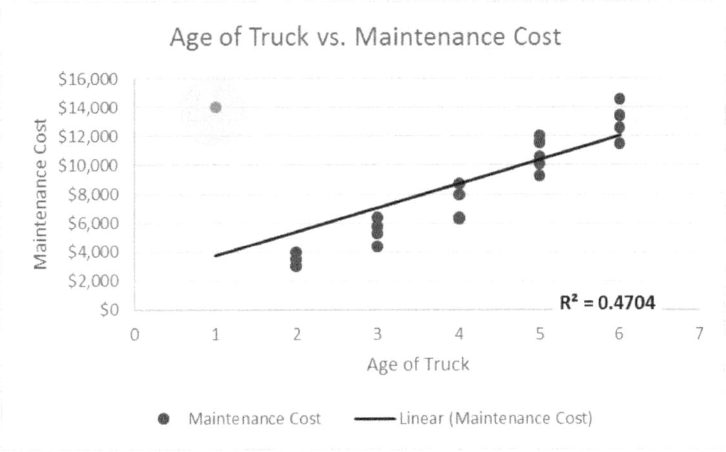

A second method of identifying outliers is through the use of box and whisker plots. Please refer to the Box and Whisker Plots section in Chapter 3 to learn more about using them to identify outliers.

Dealing With Text Data

Text data must be converted to binary data before it can be used in correlation or regression analysis. Binary data is 0s and 1s. This section describes the procedure to convert text data to binary data.

Converting Textual Data Into Binary Data

- In order to binary encode text data, we need to create a column of data for each unique text value in the text column(s) that we wish to encode except one value, which will be defined as the base value. Best practice is to define the text value that shows up first alphabetically as the base value.

- Notice the example in Table 4, we want to use the "Manufacturer" text column in a regression model
  - Note that there are three unique values in the "Manufacturer" column, "Samsung," "Sharp," and "Sony."
  - Set "Samsung" as the base and create two columns, one for "Sharp" and one for "Sony" and use an IF statement to define the 0s and 1s for the correct rows.

TABLE 4 Example Binary Encoding of Manufacturer Using "Samsung" as the Base

	A	B	C	D
1	**Manufacturer**	**Sharp**	**Sony**	**Price**
2	Sharp	1	0	$ 1,473.00
3	Samsung	0	0	$ 2,300.00
4	Samsung	0	0	$ 1,790.00
5	Sony	0	1	$ 1,250.00
6	Sharp	1	0	$ 1,546.50
7	Samsung	0	0	$ 1,922.50
8	Samsung	0	0	$ 1,372.00
9	Sharp	1	0	$ 1,149.50
10	Sharp	1	0	$ 2,000.00
11	Formulas from B2 and C2	=IF($A2=B$1,1,0)	=IF($A2=C$1,1,0)	

Simple Regression

Why study regression? Identifying and studying relationships between variables can provide information on ways to increase profits, methods to decrease costs, or variables to predict demand.

Basic Definitions I

- In regression analysis, the independent variable (X) is used to estimate the dependent variable (Y).
- The relationship between the variables is assumed to be linear.
- Both variables must be at least interval scale.
- The least squares criterion is used to determine the equation.
- Regression Equation is an equation that expresses the linear relationship between two variables.
- Least Squares Principle is used to determine a regression equation by minimizing the sum of the squares of the vertical distances between the actual Y values and the predicted values of Y.

Assumptions Underlying Linear Regression

- For each value of X, there is a group of Y values, and these Y values are normally distributed. The means of these normal distributions of Y values all lie on the straight line of regression.
- The standard deviations of these normal distributions are equal.
- The Y values are statistically independent. This means that in the selection of a sample, the Y values chosen for a particular X value do not depend on the Y values for any other X values.

General Form of the Simple Linear Regression Equation: $\hat{Y} = A + BX$

Where

- $\hat{Y}$ read Y hat, is the estimated value of the Y variable for a selected X value.
- A is the Y-intercept. It is the estimated value of Y when X = 0. Another way to put it is: A is the estimated value of Y where the regression line crosses the Y-axis when X is zero.
- B is the slope of the line, or the average change in $\hat{Y}$ for each change of one unit (either increase or decrease) in the independent variable X.
- X is any value of the independent variable that is selected.

Computing the Intercept and Slope

- For simple linear regression, the regression equation can be obtained by creating a scatterplot of the independent (X) values on the X axis and the dependent (Y) values on the Y axis, then adding a trend line and displaying the equation on the chart. The displayed equation will be the regression equation but formatted as Y = Bx + A. Refer to Figure 5 for an example regression equation on a scatter plot.
- For a full analysis, run the "Regression" tool in the Excel DATP and follow the instructions in the Multiple Regression Analysis area of this document.

Simple Regression Problem and Solution Example

Using the problem and data for the Age of Truck vs. Maintenance Costs presented in Table 3, we can run a simple regression and use the result to estimate maintenance costs based on the age of trucks as follows.

- Start by opening the Data Analysis ToolPak in Excel and then selecting "Regression."
- A dialog box will open as shown in Figure 7.
- Load the values from the Maint. Cost column into the "Input Y Range" and the values from the Age of Truck column into the "Input X Range."
- Select "Labels" if including column headers in the input range. Recommend including the headers.
- If using a standard Alpha of 5% leave the "Confidence Level" at 95%. Alpha is related to the confidence level with the equation Alpha = 1 – Confidence Level, so if you decide to use a different Alpha then you will need to adjust the confidence level accordingly.

- Leave "Constant is Zero" unchecked, checking this box forces the intercept of the regression line to zero. There is an open debate among researchers as to whether or not the intercept should be forced to zero if it is found to be insignificant. The authors of this book are on the "do not force the intercept to zero" side of this argument.
- Select an appropriate cell to place the output and press OK to create the regression results.

FIGURE 7 Excel's Data Analysis ToolPak Regression Dialog Box

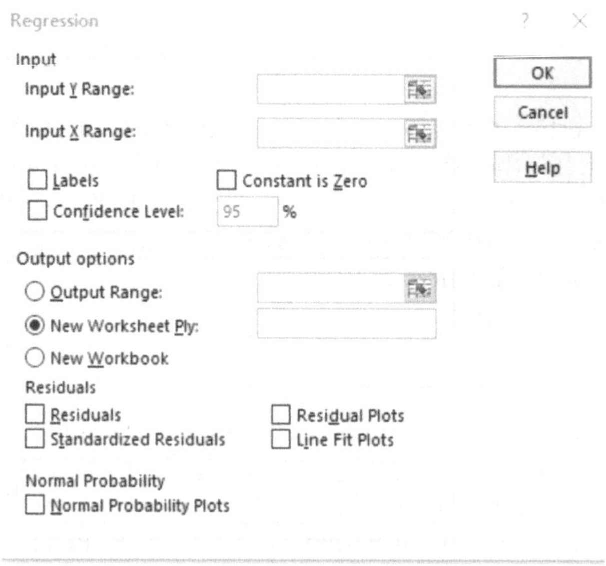

- Selected portions of the regression output are shown in Table 5. The "Global Test" information was added to the regression output to show that the null hypothesis of all of the coefficients (B_i) are equal to zero can be rejected in this case. The Significance F and P-values were also formatted as percentages and conditional formatting was added to show the P-values are in fact less than Alpha (5%).

TABLE 5 Regression Output for Age of Truck vs. Maint. Cost Problem

SUMMARY OUTPUT

Regression Statistics	
Multiple R	0.966064009
R Square	0.933279669
Adjusted R Square	0.930102511
Standard Error	1013.354616
Observations	23

ANOVA			Global Test		
	df	*F*	*Significance F*	*Inequality*	*Alpha*
Regression	1	293.7466423	0.000000000008%	<	5%
Residual	21		Reject Ho: coefficient is not equal 0		
Total	22				

	Coefficients	*P-value*	*Lower 95%*	*Upper 95%*
Intercept (A)	-1652.30756	1.521%	-2952.385901	-352.229219
Age of Truck (B)	2441.379725	0.000%	2145.147993	2737.611457

Using the coefficients from the regression output shown in Table 5, we can estimate maintenance costs for other trucks of given ages as shown in Table 6. Therefore, for a 3.5-year-old truck we would estimate the annual maintenance costs to be between $4,865 and $8,919 with the most likely value to be $6,893. In addition, for a 4.5-year-old truck we would estimate the annual maintenance costs to be between $7,307 and $11,360 with the most likely value to be $9,334.

TABLE 6 Simple Regression Model Estimates

	A	B	C	D
1	**Regression Equation Estimates**			
2	**Age of Truck (X)**	**Lower 95 PI**	**Estimated Maint. Cost (Y_{hat})**	**Upper 95 PI**
3	3.5	$4,865.81	$6,893	$8,919.23
4	4.5	$7,307.19	$9,334	$11,360.61
5	Formulas from row 3	=C3-2*$C$8	=$A$8+$B$8*A3	=C3+2*$C$8
6				
7	**Intercept (A)**	**Age of Truck (B)**	**Standard Error**	
8	-1652.30756	$2,441.38	$1,013	

Video Available: Watch the Chapter 6—Simple Regression Video

Multiple Regression

Basic Definitions I

- $X_1 \ldots X_k$ are the independent variables
- A is the Y-intercept
- B_1 is the coefficient of X_1. It is the net change in Y for each unit change in X_1 holding $X_2 \ldots X_k$ constant. It is called a partial regression coefficient or just a regression coefficient of X_1. A regression coefficient (B_i) is computed for each independent X variable.
- The least squares criterion is used to develop this equation.
- Determining B_1, B_2, and so forth is very tedious, we will use the Excel DATP to calculate them.
- The multiple standard error of estimate is a measure of the effectiveness of the regression equation. It is measured in the same units as the dependent variable.

The Multiple Regression Equation is: $\hat{Y} = A + B_1X_1 + B_2X_2 + B_3X_3 + \ldots + B_kX_k$

Multiple Regression and Correlation Assumptions

- The independent variables and the dependent variable have a linear relationship. The dependent variable must be continuous and at least interval-scale.
- The residual must be the same for all values of Y. When this is the case, we say the difference exhibits homoscedasticity.
- The residuals should follow the normal distributed with mean 0.
- Successive values of the dependent variable must be uncorrelated.

Coefficient of Multiple Determination (R^2)

- The Coefficient of Multiple determination is the percent of variation in the dependent variable $\hat{Y}$, explained by the set of independent variables, $X_1, X_2, X_3, \ldots X_k$.
- Symbolized by R^2.
- Ranges from 0 to 1.
- Cannot assume negative values.

The Adjusted R^2

- The number of independent variables in a multiple regression equation makes the coefficient of determination larger.
- If the number of variables, k, and the sample size, n, are equal, the coefficient of determination is 1.0.
- To balance the effect that the number of independent variables has on the coefficient of multiple determination, adjusted R^2 is used instead.

Global Test: Testing the Multiple Regression Model

- The global test is used to investigate whether any of the independent variables have significant coefficients.
- The null hypothesis H_0 is: all of the coefficients (B_i) are equal to zero.
- The alternate hypothesis H_1 is: at least one coefficient (B_i) is not equal to zero.
- The decision rule is to Reject H_0 if the Significance F is less than Alpha. Common practice is to set Alpha to 0.05 in Regression tests; however, other values of Alpha could be used if desired.

Evaluating Individual Regression Coefficients (B_i)

- This test is used to determine which independent variables have nonzero regression coefficients.
- The variables that have zero regression coefficients are usually dropped from the analysis.
- The null hypothesis for each coefficient (B_i) is $B_i = 0$.
- The alternate hypothesis for each coefficient (B_i) is $B_i \neq 0$.
- The decision rule is to Reject H_0 if the p-value is less than Alpha.

Analyzing the Output

- Conduct and document the Global Test
  - The global test is used to investigate whether any of the independent variables have significant coefficients.
  - The null hypothesis H_0 is: all of the coefficients (B_i) are equal to zero.
  - The alternate hypothesis H_1 is: at least one coefficient (B_i) is not equal to zero.
  - The decision rule is to Reject H_0 if the Significance F is less than Alpha.
  - A good way to word cases where H_0 is rejected would be: "Reject H0: At least one coefficient is not equal to zero."
- Conduct and document the Individual Tests
  - This test is used to determine which independent variables have nonzero regression coefficients.
  - The variables that have zero regression coefficients are dropped from the reduced model.
  - The null hypothesis for each coefficient (B_i) is $B_i = 0$.
  - The alternate hypothesis for each coefficient (B_i) is $B_i \neq 0$.
  - The decision rule is to Reject H_0 if the p-value is less than Alpha.
- Review the Adjusted R Square: R^2 varies between 0 and 1. A value of 0 indicates zero predictive value, while a 1 indicates perfect prediction. Therefore higher values generally indicate a better model.
- Review the Standard Error: the standard error is in the same dimensions as the predicted variable and indicates the range over which estimates of Y will vary. Therefore smaller values generally indicate a better model.

Removing Insignificant Variables

- Based on the results of your Individual Tests, remove the insignificant variables from the regression model
  - If "All at Once" reduction is requested or desired, remove all independent "X" variable columns that were previously identified as "not significant" from the data by making a copy of the data and removing the "not significant" columns. Re-run the regression tool using the reduced data as input.
  - If "Backward" reduction is requested or desired, remove the most "insignificant" variable, the variable with the highest p-value, from the data by making a copy of the data and removing the correct column. Re-run the regression tool using the reduced data as input. Next analyze this regression output, remove the next most "insignificant" variable from the data by making a copy of the data and removing the correct column. Repeat this procedure until all variables are "Significant" (i.e., all p-values < Alpha).
  - Please note that other variable selection methods such as "Forward Selection," "Stepwise Selection/Elimination," "Sequential Replacement," and "Best Subsets" are commonly used but are beyond the scope of this book because they are rather difficult to implement in Excel.

Building the Regression Equation

- Using the regression equation : $\hat{Y} = A + B_1X_1 + B_2X_2 + B_3X_3 + \ldots + B_kX_k$
- Create estimated values for the dependent variable "$\hat{Y}$" for the given input independent values "X."
- A = the coefficient of the Intercept given in the regression output.
- B_i = the coefficients of the independent values given in the regression output.
- Regression equations can be built using either the full model or reduced model output or both.

Building the Prediction Intervals

- A prediction interval estimate is a range of values centered around $\hat{Y}$
- This range encompasses 95% of the probability of $\hat{Y}$ occurring within the lower bound to upper bound range.
- The lower bound of the prediction interval is $\hat{Y}$ - 2SE.
- The upper bound of the prediction interval is $\hat{Y}$ + 2SE.
- 2*SE assumes alpha was set to 5%, this yields **approximately** a 95% prediction interval.
- Where SE is the Standard Error as listed in the DATP output.

Multiple Regression Stepwise Procedure

FIGURE 8 Multiple Regression Stepwise Procedure

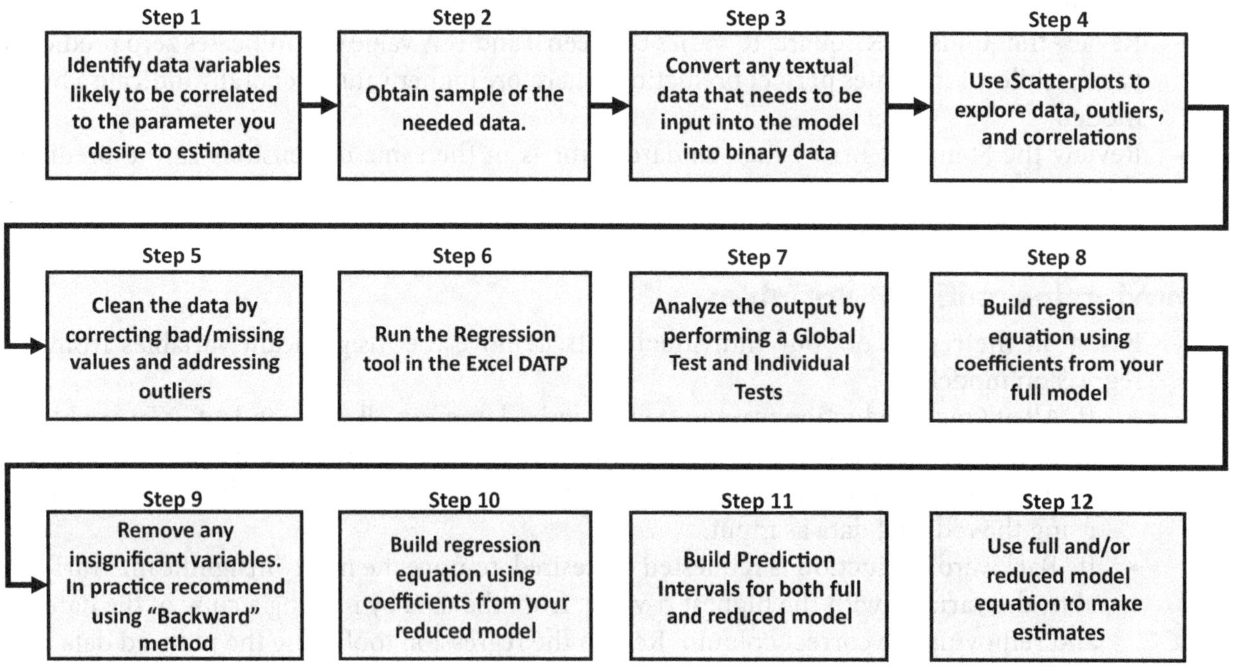
Step 1
Identify data variables likely to be correlated to the parameter you desire to estimate
Step 2
Obtain sample of the needed data.
Step 3
Convert any textual data that needs to be input into the model into binary data
Step 4
Use Scatterplots to explore data, outliers, and correlations
Step 5
Clean the data by correcting bad/missing values and addressing outliers
Step 6
Run the Regression tool in the Excel DATP
Step 7
Analyze the output by performing a Global Test and Individual Tests
Step 8
Build regression equation using coefficients from your full model
Step 9
Remove any insignificant variables. In practice recommend using "Backward" method
Step 10
Build regression equation using coefficients from your reduced model
Step 11
Build Prediction Intervals for both full and reduced model
Step 12
Use full and/or reduced model equation to make estimates

Multiple Regression Problem and Solution Example

A professional baseball team is in a bad slump (i.e., losing streak). Ticket sales are plummeting and the Director of Sports Operations is looking for ways to generate more revenue at the gate. Data from the last 30 weeks has been collected in terms of the number of fans in attendance (i.e., gate receipts). In addition to this attendance, data has been collected in terms of sources of promotions and advertising (i.e., two for one promotions, television advertising budgets, and radio advertising budgets). The data is shown below. The director would like to know how the forms of advertising influences gate receipts. Develop a multi-linear regression model to predict gate receipts.

TABLE 7 Data for Multiple Regression Example Problem

Week	Two for One Promotion	Promotion Encoded	Television Advertising	Radio Advertising	Radio Advertising ^2	Gate Receipts
1	N	0	$60,000	$30,000	$900,000,000	$620,000
2	N	0	$75,000	$35,000	$1,225,000,000	$750,000
3	Y	1	$98,000	$87,000	$7,569,000,000	$950,000
4	N	0	$80,000	$80,000	$6,400,000,000	$780,000
5	N	0	$90,000	$100,000	$10,000,000,000	$950,000
6	Y	1	$90,000	$90,000	$8,100,000,000	$910,000
7	N	0	$70,000	$75,000	$5,625,000,000	$720,000
8	Y	1	$90,000	$98,000	$9,604,000,000	$950,000
9	Y	1	$90,000	$90,000	$8,100,000,000	$880,000
10	Y	1	$100,000	$95,000	$9,025,000,000	$970,000
11	N	0	$50,000	$50,000	$2,500,000,000	$490,000
12	N	0	$71,000	$75,000	$5,625,000,000	$700,000
13	N	0	$75,000	$80,000	$6,400,000,000	$750,000
14	N	0	$80,000	$85,000	$7,225,000,000	$780,000
15	Y	1	$90,000	$88,000	$7,744,000,000	$890,000
16	N	0	$88,000	$90,000	$8,100,000,000	$870,000
17	N	0	$80,000	$85,000	$7,225,000,000	$790,000
18	Y	1	$78,000	$85,000	$7,225,000,000	$850,000
19	N	0	$60,000	$60,000	$3,600,000,000	$570,000
20	N	0	$80,000	$80,000	$6,400,000,000	$810,000
21	N	0	$75,000	$80,000	$6,400,000,000	$760,000
22	Y	1	$88,000	$90,000	$8,100,000,000	$880,000
23	Y	1	$80,000	$85,000	$7,225,000,000	$830,000
24	Y	1	$100,000	$95,000	$9,025,000,000	$970,000
25	N	0	$58,000	$65,000	$4,225,000,000	$600,000
26	N	0	$86,000	$80,000	$6,400,000,000	$840,000
27	Y	1	$91,000	$90,000	$8,100,000,000	$870,000
28	Y	1	$99,000	$90,000	$8,100,000,000	$950,000
29	N	0	$70,000	$70,000	$4,900,000,000	$640,000
30	Y	1	$79,000	$75,000	$5,625,000,000	$800,000

Note: The "Two for One Promotion" data has already been binary encoded, no (N) was assigned as the base and yes (Y) was assigned a value of 1.

At this point, we are at step 4 of the solution and we will next show scatterplots of the independent variables (promotion and advertising) versus the dependent variable (gate receipts).

FIGURE 9 Scatterplot of Two for One Promotion vs. Gate Receipts. The coefficient of determination is 45.36%. No bad data or significant outliers were identified.

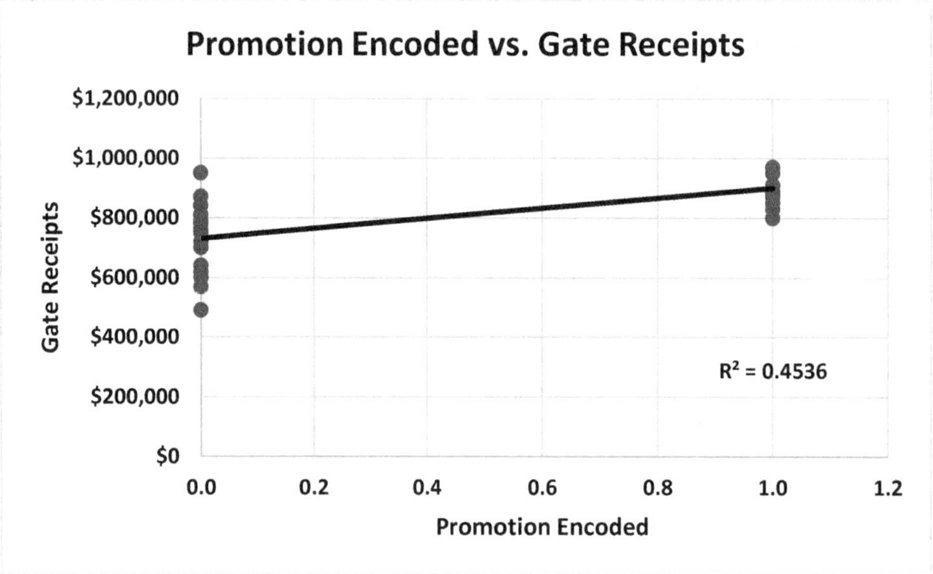

FIGURE 10 Scatterplot of Television Advertising vs. Gate Receipts. The coefficient of determination is 10.32%. Using this chart, a significant outlier was found in week 12, a television advertising budget of $210,000 was recorded. Research revealed that the actual TV advertising budget for week 12 was $71,000.

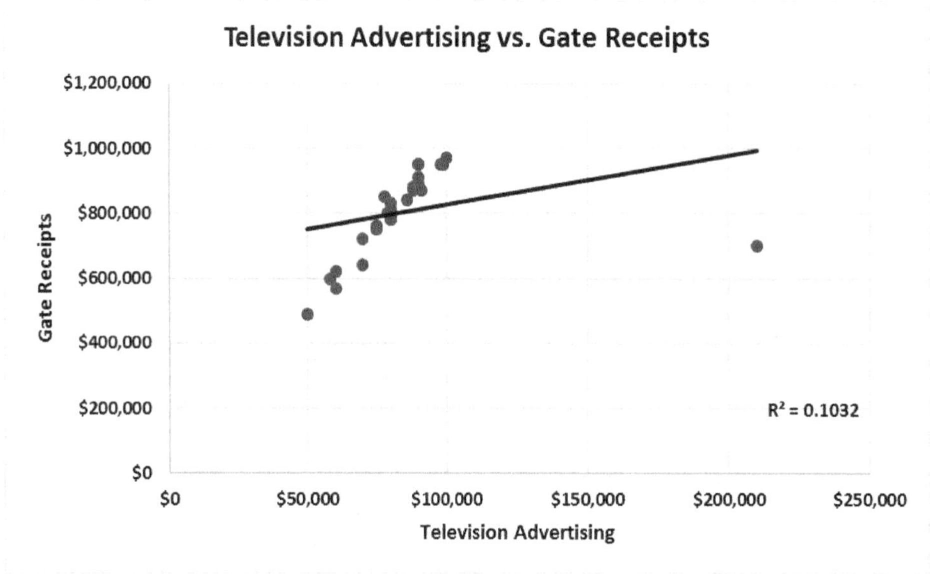

FIGURE 11 Scatterplot of Television Advertising vs. Gate Receipts after week 12 television advertising budget was corrected. The coefficient of determination is now 94.88%. The corrected data will be used in the regression analysis.

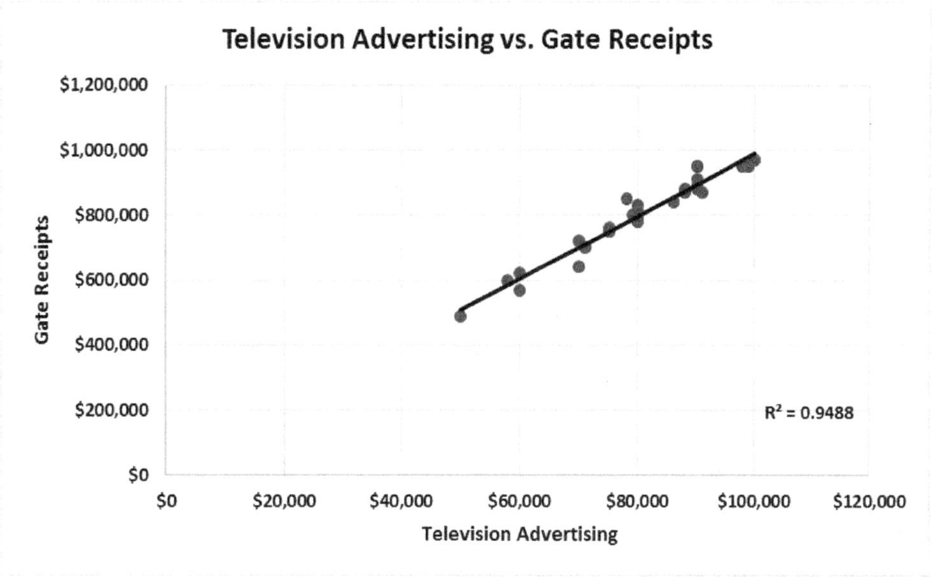

FIGURE 12 Scatterplot of Radio Advertising vs. Gate Receipts. Notice the curved shape of the plots, a polynomial trend line best describes this relationship; this suggests that adding a squared term for Radio Advertising would be appropriate. With the polynomial trend line the coefficient of determination is 85.54%.

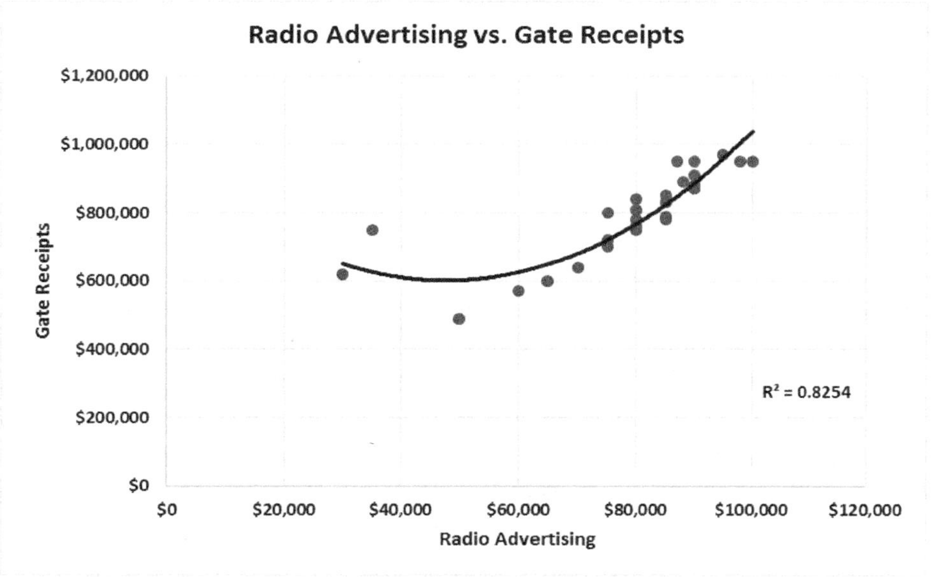

TABLE 8 Selected DATP Regression Output (from step 6 of the stepwise procedure)

SUMMARY OUTPUT

Regression Statistics	
Multiple R	98.3%
R Square	96.7%
Adjusted R Square	96.2%
Standard Error	24743
Observations	30

ANOVA			
	df	*F*	*Significance F*
Regression	4	184.1	3.72611E-18
Residual	25		
Total	29		

	Coefficients	*P-value*	*Lower 95%*	*Upper 95%*
Intercept	313751.549	0.1%	133247.0	494256.1
Promotion Encoded	12863.377	29.9%	-12105.7	37832.4
Television Advertising	7.173	0.0%	5.6	8.8
Radio Advertising	-5.623	0.9%	-9.7	-1.5
Radio Advertising ^2	0.00005	0.3%	0.0	0.0

Step 7 is to perform a global test, the Significance F shown in the regression output is 3.72611E-18 which is much smaller than Alpha (5%), therefore we can reject the null hypothesis and conclude that at least one coefficient (B_i) is not equal to zero. Also in Step 7 is the requirement to perform individual tests for each regression coefficient. In the regression output, we note that the P-value of the Promotion Encoded term is greater than Alpha (5%). Therefore, we conclude that the Promotion Encoded term coefficient is not significant and that term should be dropped from the reduced regression model. In addition, since the P-value of the Television Advertising, Radio Advertising, and Radio Advertising Squared are less than Alpha (5%), we can also conclude that their coefficients are significant and not equal to zero. Note, in this output the Intercept P-value is less than 5.0%; however, we want to always leave the Intercept in the regression analysis even in a case where the Intercept P-value is greater than Alpha.

Step 8 is to build the regression equation using the coefficients from the full model regression output. In Table 9, we have copied the intercept and independent variable coefficients from the DATP output in row 8.

- The estimated gate receipts for four different promotion and advertising budgets are calculated using the regression equation:

$$\hat{Y} = A + B_1X_1 + B_2X_2 + B_3X_3 + \ldots + B_kX_k$$

where A is the intercept coefficient, B1 is the promotion encoded coefficient, X1 is the promotion encoded point value, B2 is the television advertising coefficient, X2 is the television advertising point value, B3 is the radio advertising coefficient, X3 is the radio advertising point value, B4 is the radio advertising squared coefficient, X4 is the radio advertising squared point value.

- The lower and upper 95% Prediction Intervals are calculated using the equation

$$\pm 95\ PI = PE \pm 2SE$$

where PE is the point estimate, estimated gate receipts in this case, and SE is the standard error.

TABLE 9 Full Model Estimates of Gate Receipts along with lower and upper 95% prediction intervals using the regression output from Excel's DATP.

	A	B	C	D	E	F	G	H
1	**Two for One Promotion**	**Promotion Encoded**	**Television Advertising**	**Radio Advertising**	**Radio Advertising ^2**	**-95% PI**	**Est. Gate Receipts**	**+95% PI**
2	N	0	$92,000	$42,000	$1,764,000,000	$782,604	$832,090	$881,576
3	Y	1	$61,000	$90,000	$8,100,000,000	$642,899	$692,385	$692,385
4	Y	1	$74,000	$70,000	$4,900,000,000	$677,044	$726,530	$726,530
5	N	0	$68,000	$44,000	$1,936,000,000	$608,426	$657,912	$657,912
6								
7	**Intercept**	**Promotion Encoded**	**Television Advertising**	**Radio Advertising**	**Radio Advertising ^2**	**Standard Error**		
8	313751.55	12863.38	7.17	-5.62	0.00	24742.99		
9								
10	Promotion Encoded formula (cell B2):				=IF(A2="Y",1,0)			
11	Estimated Gate Receipts formula (cell G2):				=$A$8+SUMPRODUCT($B$8:$E$8,B2:E2)			
12	-95% PI: (cell F2):				=G2-2*$F$8			
13	+95% PI: (cell H2):				=G2+2*$F$8			

Step 9 is to remove any insignificant variables, in this problem the "Promotion Encoded" independent variable was identified as insignificant so we remove this variable from the input and run the DATP regression tool without it.

TABLE 10 Selected DATP Regression Output (Step 9: Reduced Model Output)

SUMMARY OUTPUT

Regression Statistics	
Multiple R	98.3%
R Square	96.6%
Adjusted R Square	96.2%
Standard Error	24803
Observations	30

ANOVA			
	df	*F*	*Significance F*
Regression	3	243.9	3.76522E-19
Residual	26		
Total	29		

	Coefficients	*P-value*	*Lower 95%*	*Upper 95%*
Intercept	294922.000	0.2%	118074.6	471769.4
Television Advertising	7.488	0.0%	6.0	9.0
Radio Advertising	-5.676	0.8%	-9.8	-1.6
Radio Advertising ^2	0.000	0.3%	0.0	0.0

TABLE 11 Reduced Model Estimates of Gate Receipts along with lower and upper 95% prediction intervals using the regression output from Excel's DATP.

	A	B	C	D	E	F	G	H
1	**Two for One Promotion**	**Promotion Encoded**	**Television Advertising**	**Radio Advertising**	**Radio Advertising ^2**	**-95% CI**	**Est. Gate Receipts**	**+95% CI**
2	N	0	$92,000.00	$42,000.00	$1,764,000,000	$791,273	$840,879	$890,484
3	Y	1	$61,000.00	$90,000.00	$8,100,000,000	$629,460	$679,065	$728,671
4	Y	1	$74,000.00	$70,000.00	$4,900,000,000	$667,209	$716,815	$766,420
5	N	0	$68,000.00	$44,000.00	$1,936,000,000	$609,506	$659,112	$708,717
6								
7	**Intercept**	**Promotion Encoded**	**Television Advertising**	**Radio Advertising**	**Radio Advertising ^2**	**Standard Error**		
8	294922.00	0.00	7.49	-5.68	0.00	24802.75		
9								
10	Promotion Encoded formula (cell B2):		=IF(A2="Y",1,0)					
11	Estimated Gate Receipts formula (cell G2):		=$A$8+SUMPRODUCT($B$8:$E$8,B2:E2)					
12	-95% PI: (cell F2):		=G2-2*$F$8					
13	+95% PI: (cell H2):		=G2+2*$F$8					

In summary, a regression equation using prior television and radio advertising budgets can be built and used to estimate gate receipts for various proposed future television and radio advertising budgets with a margin of error of around $100,000.

CHAPTER 7

PREDICTIVE ANALYTICS
Time Series

In this chapter, we introduce time series analysis and forecasting. A time series is nothing more than data collected and ordered by time (i.e., day, month, and year). Time series forecasting is a special subset of predictive analytics due to the characteristics that we see within the data we are trying to model. For example, consider a lawn mower manufacturer who wants to build a forecasting model that predicts the demand for a certain lawnmower given the month of the year. We would expect customers to buy more lawn mowers in the spring and summer than we would in the fall and winter. However, we might also see a year-to-year increase in sales. From this simple example, if we were to plot the data, we might see a positive trend and another characteristic of the data called seasonality. The seasonality characteristic would show cyclic behavior. In other words, we might see peaks and valleys similar to a sinusoidal wave. In addition based on the positive trend, we might also see the "waves" getting larger and larger as time progresses. We consider time series a special subset of predictive analytics simply because of the "shape" of the data we are trying to model. For example, linear regression would not be a suitable model to capture seasonal behavior. Thus, we need to resort to other methods that are suitable for capturing this type of behavior.

From a business perspective, time series forecasts are very important because they allow businesses to anticipate changes that they might have to make within the organization. For example, a business could analyze time series data in order to develop quarterly forecasts of sales for products that they plan to manufacture and sell over the next year. Production schedules, raw material purchasing, inventory, and sales quotas will all be affected by the quarterly forecasts so accurately forecasting time series data is extremely important for an organization's well-being. Consequently, poor forecasts may result in poor planning and increased costs for the company.

A TIME SERIES is a collection of data recorded over a period of time (daily, weekly, monthly, or quarterly), that can be used by management to compute forecasts as input to planning and decision-making. It usually assumes past patterns will continue into the future. (Lind, 2015)

Components of a Time Series

- **Secular Trend:** the smooth long-term direction of a time series
- **Cyclical Variation:** the rise and fall of a time series over periods longer than one year
- **Seasonal Variation:** patterns of change in a time series within a year which tends to repeat each year
- **Irregular Variation:** classified into two categories (episodic or residual)
  - **Episodic**: unpredictable but identifiable
  - **Residual**: also called chance fluctuation and unidentifiable

Secular Trend

The longest-term trend that we find in a time series is called the "**Secular Trend.**" This long-term change to relatively higher or lower values is usually the result of long-term factors such as population changes, changing consumer preferences, changes in technology, inflation, and so on. For example, the number of associates at Home Depot, Inc. increased quickly during the 1990s and early 2000s as the company was rapidly expanding; however, this trend changed in 2007 with the major economic recession in the US. Since that time, the secular trend has been showing a much smaller rate of growth (Lind, 2015). As we can see in the chart below, we need to be very careful when using time series data to make assumptions and/or forecasts about future values. Factors within and outside of the company could have very large effects on future trends. The quicker we can recognize these changing patterns, the better we become at making business decisions.

FIGURE 1 Example of Changes in Associates due to Secular Trend

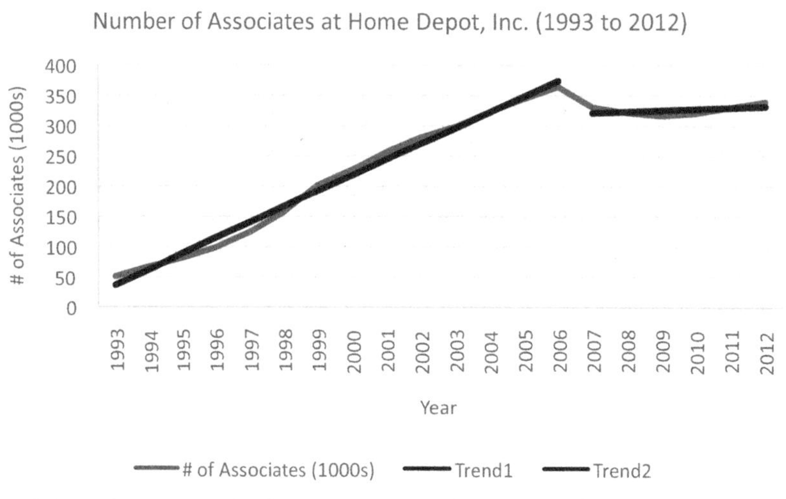

Cyclical Variations

The next trend timescale is "**Cyclical Variations.**" This variation shows the rise and fall of a time series over periods longer than one year. These variations are often associated with the expansion and recession cycles that we see in modern economies. Individual market sectors also go through the business cycles. For example, the oil and gas industry is widely known for its extreme boom and bust cycles. Figure 2 shows how a company's sales often increase during times of economic expansion and decrease during times of economic recession. Quickly recognizing a coming switch in this pattern and planning for the associated changes can result in significant reduction in losses and/or increased profits as the market conditions change. For example, during the major recession of 2007–2008, General Motors failed to be well enough prepared to weather the recession while Ford Motors had planned well for the rainy day. The result was that General Motors had to go through bankruptcy and only survived through government assistance while Ford Motors continued operations though at a greatly reduced rate of production.

FIGURE 2 Example of Changes in Sales due to Cyclical Variation

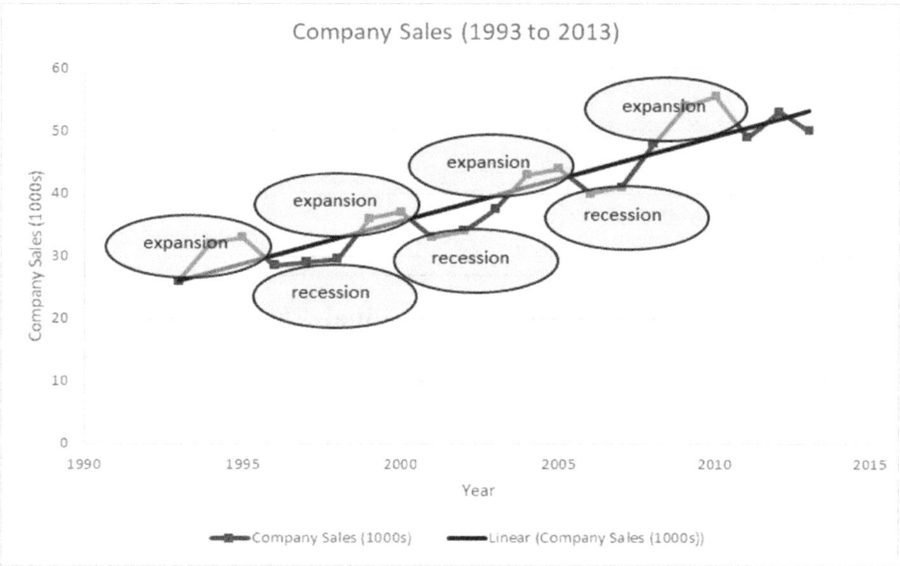

Seasonal Variations

The next trend timescale is "**Seasonal Variations.**" These variations show the rise and fall of a time series over periods of one year. These variations are often associated with the business sectors having large changes in sales over the different seasons of the year. For example, a ski resort may receive 90% or more of its total revenue during the winter season while a mowing service would only have business over the summer. These businesses often attempt to branch out into other areas in order to earn revenue during their off-seasons. A ski resort may open a downhill mountain biking course while a mowing business may clear snow in the winter. Figure 3 on the following page shows how a lawn equipment company's sales increase during the mowing season and then drop significantly during the fall and winter. By properly forecasting the next year's seasonal variations, a company can plan for such important items as production, marketing, inventory, hiring, transportation, and so on.

FIGURE 3 Example of Changes in Sales due to Seasonal Variation

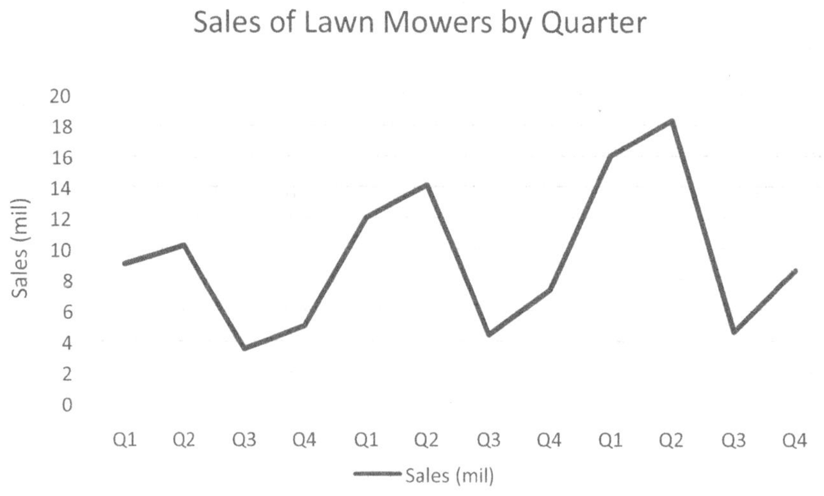

Irregular Variations

Irregular variations are classified into **episodic** and **residual**. These types of variation are seemingly random occurring variations that happen in all processes and environments. Some of these variations can often be tracked to a particular event. For example, a heat wave over a ski resort may significantly affect their revenue just as a summer drought could reduce the revenue for a mowing service company. While these events are at times identifiable, they are unpredictable. Therefore, time series methods attempt to remove these variations from the model before using the other types of trends in building a forecast. However, it should be noted that all forecasts will be affected by these irregular variations and the accuracy will be reduced because of them.

Simple Moving Averages

A moving average is a critical calculation in the development of a time series forecast. It helps to reduce the irregular variations or noise in the data and helps to reveal patterns that we would not otherwise see. Charting the moving average is used to make sense of the data and markets by showing the data in a visual way. In financial markets, moving averages are used very heavily to help rationalize the market.

A moving average is useful in smoothing a time series to see its trend. (Lind, 2015)

The Simple Moving Average (SMA) is perhaps the oldest and most widely used technical indicator in financial applications. What makes it a favorite of investors is the "simple" signals it gives. The SMA is calculated by summing the data over a given number of periods, then dividing the sum by the number of periods. For example, a 150-day SMA would sum together the stock closing prices for the last 150 days, and then divide that by the number of prices summed. The AVERAGE function in Excel is very useful to build an SMA. Each new day would drop the 150th value and add the new value so the average moves through time. SMAs are reactionary indicators meaning that they do not future predict price movements. The shorter the SMA the more sensitive it is to new price changes.

In financial applications, a Simple Moving Average (SMA) is the mean of the previous n values. However, in other applications, the SMA is the mean of an equal number of data on either side of a central value. We will call this second SMA a Central Moving Average (CMA).

FIGURE 4 Example of a 150-Day and 50-Day SMA for Apple's Closing Price Over a Six-Month Period

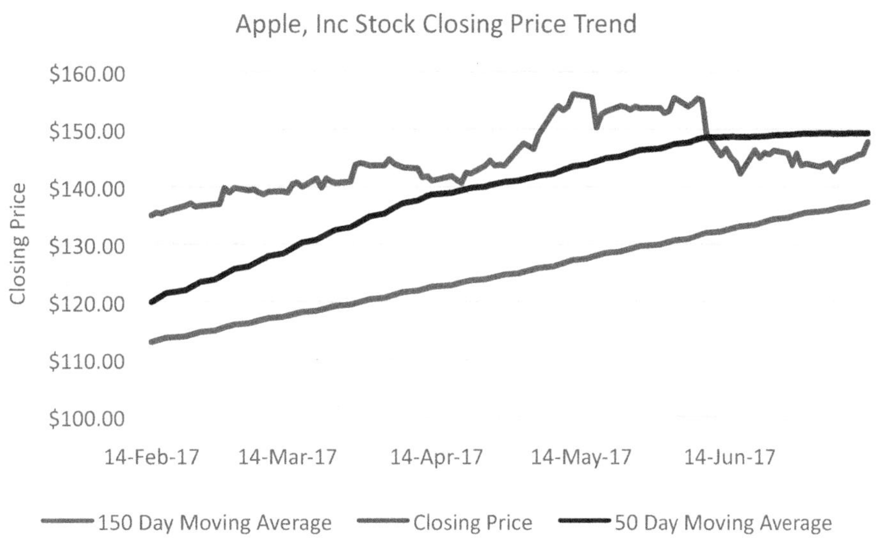

Video Available: Watch the Chapter 7—Moving Averages video

Weighted Moving Averages

A weighted moving average is a moving average that assigns more weight to recent observations and less weight to older observations. There are many techniques that can be used to weight the observations. However, they should follow the following formula.

$$WMA = \frac{\Sigma_{i=1}^{n} Observations_i * Weights_i}{\Sigma_{i=1}^{n} Weights_i}$$

Where n is the number of observations in the moving average and the number of weights. In Excel this formula is:

$$WMA = \frac{SUMPRODUCT(Observations, Weights)}{SUM(Weights)}$$

Please note that if the sum of the weights is 1.0 then the denominator can be ignored.

FIGURE 5 Example of a 20-Day SMA and 20-Day WMA for Microsoft's Closing Price Over a Six-Month Period

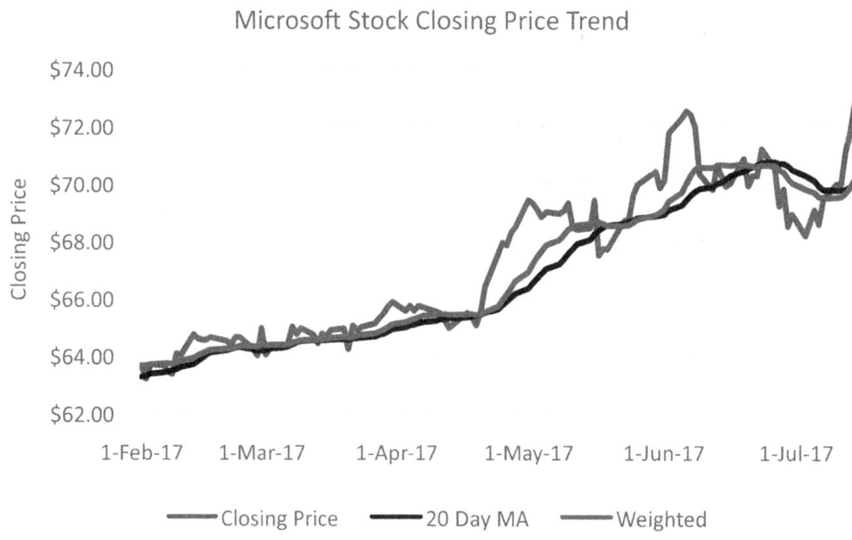

Weighted moving averages are more sensitive to recent changes and less sensitive to older changes and therefore some investors prefer them to simple moving averages.

Video Available: Watch the Chapter 7—Weighted Moving Averages video

Forecasting Using Exponential Smoothing

One method of forecasting using time series data is Exponential Smoothing. Exponential smoothing is a method of weighted moving average that calculates the average of a time series by giving recent observations more weight than earlier observations based on a smoothing parameter called alpha. The equation for the forecast is:

$$F_t = \alpha A_{t-1} + (1+\alpha)F_{t-1}$$

This equation requires only three items of data

- The last period's forecast
- The observation for this period
- A smoothing parameter, alpha (α), where $0 \leq \alpha \leq 1.0$

Where

- F_t is the forecast value for the upcoming period t
- α is the smoothing constant
- A_{t-1} is the previous period's actual observation
- F_{t-1} is the previous period's forecast value

Exponential Smoothing Characteristics

- The emphasis given to the most recent observations can be adjusted by changing the smoothing parameter
- Larger α values emphasize recent observations and result in forecasts more responsive to changes in the underlying average
- Smaller α values treat past observations more uniformly and result in more stable forecasts
- When the underlying average is changing, results will lag actual changes

Exponential Smoothing Problem and Solution Example

A company would like to use time series data on their weekly product demand to forecast their demand for the upcoming week. Develop an exponential smoothing forecast for week 20 given the actual demand for the 19 weeks as shown below using alpha of 0.60.

TABLE 1 Weekly Demand and Forecast Demands

	A	C	D
1	**Alpha (α)**	0.6	
2	**Initial Forecast**	64	
3			
4	**Week**	**Actual Demand**	**Forecast Demand**
5	1	58	64.0
6	2	62	60.4
7	3	67	61.4
8	4	64	64.7
9	5	69	64.3
10	6	71	67.1
11	7	72	69.4
12	8	75	71.0
13	9	77	73.4
14	10	79	75.6
15	11	81	77.6
16	12	83	79.6
17	13	86	81.7
18	14	89	84.3
19	15	87	87.1
20	16	91	87.0
21	17	90	89.4
22	18	93	89.8
23	19	94	91.7
24	20	Forecast Period	93.1
25	Forecast Equation (cell C6)		=$B$1*B5+(1-$B$1)*C5

FIGURE 6 Actual Demand Line vs. Forecast Demand Line, for Example, Exponential Smoothing Example Problem

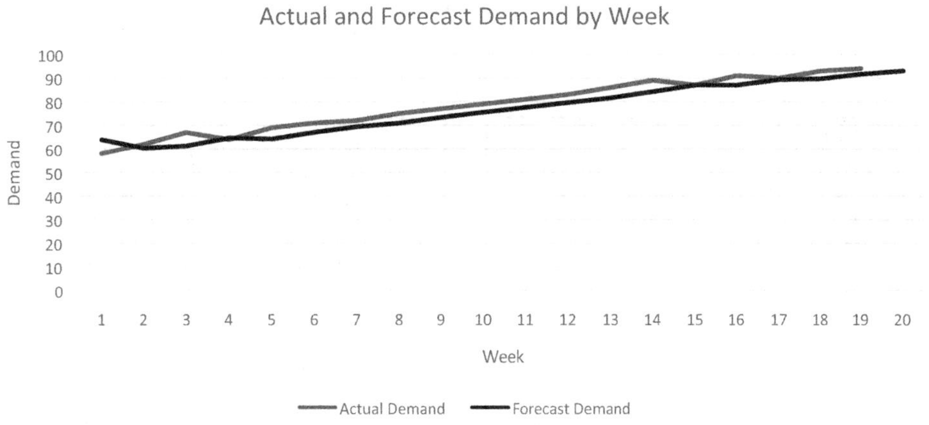

Video Available: Watch the Chapter 7—Exponential Smoothing video

Forecasting Using Time Series

Developing a Time Series Forecast is a multi-step process and is best used for data that has a clear seasonal or cyclical trend. The basic concept is to use regression to find the linear secular trend and moving averages to find the seasonal or cyclical trend and then multiply the trends together to create an equation that can be used to project the needed values forward in time.

The Time Forecast equation is

$$Y_t = Secular_t * Seasonal_t$$

The step-wise procedure to create a time series is

FIGURE 7 Step-wise procedure for developing a time series forecast. Note the Irregularity term is very difficult to predict and therefore this term is usually ignored

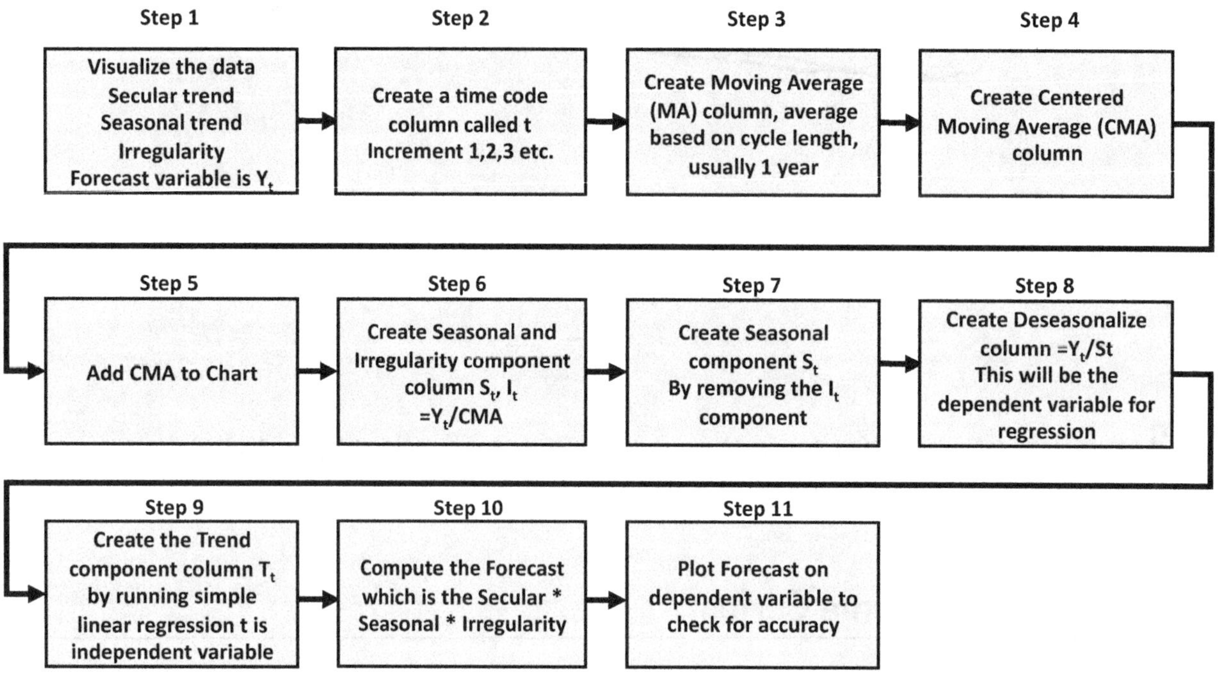

Time Series Forecast Problem and Solution Example

An auto dealership would like to use four years of previous car sales data to develop a forecast of car sales for the upcoming year. The sales data and forecast values are shown below.

TABLE 2 Example Time Series Forecast Problem and Solution

	A	B	C	D	E	F	G	H	I	J	K
1	**Quarterly Car Sales**										
2	**t**	**Year**	**Qtr**	**Sales (1000s)**	**MA (4Q)**	**CMA (4Q)**	**S_t, I_t**	**S_t**	**Y_t/S_t**	**T_t**	**Forecast**
3	1	Year 1	1	$4.8				0.93	5.15	5.25	4.89
4	2		2	$4.1				0.84	4.89	5.39	4.52
5	3		3	$6.0	$5.4	$5.5	1.10	1.09	5.49	5.54	6.06
6	4		4	$6.5	$5.6	$5.7	1.13	1.14	5.69	5.69	6.50
7	5	Year 2	1	$5.8	$5.9	$6.0	0.97	0.93	6.22	5.84	5.44
8	6		2	$5.2	$6.1	$6.2	0.84	0.84	6.21	5.98	5.01
9	7		3	$6.8	$6.3	$6.3	1.08	1.09	6.22	6.13	6.70
10	8		4	$7.4	$6.4	$6.4	1.16	1.14	6.47	6.28	7.18
11	9	Year 3	1	$6.0	$6.5	$6.5	0.92	0.93	6.44	6.42	5.99
12	10		2	$5.6	$6.6	$6.7	0.84	0.84	6.68	6.57	5.50
13	11		3	$7.5	$6.7	$6.8	1.11	1.09	6.86	6.72	7.35
14	12		4	$7.8	$6.8	$6.8	1.14	1.14	6.82	6.87	7.85
15	13	Year 4	1	$6.3	$6.9	$6.9	0.91	0.93	6.76	7.01	6.54
16	14		2	$5.9	$7.0	$7.1	0.83	0.84	7.04	7.16	6.00
17	15		3	$8.0	$7.2			1.09	7.32	7.31	7.99
18	16		4	$8.4				1.14	7.35	7.45	8.52
19	17	Year 5	1					0.93		7.60	7.09
20	18		2					0.84		7.75	6.49
21	19		3					1.09		7.90	8.63
22	20		4					1.14		8.04	9.19
23			**Formulas**								
24		**Seasonal**	MA (4Q) formula from cell E5			=AVERAGE(D3:D6)					
25	**Qtr**	**S_t Average**	CMA (4Q) formula from cell F5			=AVERAGE(E5:E6)					
26	1	0.93	S_t, I_t formula from cell G5			=D5/F5					
27	2	0.84	S_t formula from cell H3			=INDEX($A$26:$B$29, MATCH(C3,$A$26:$A$29,0),2)					
28	3	1.09	Y_t/S_t formula from cell I3			=D3/H3					
29	4	1.14	Tt formula from cell J3			=$B$52+$B$53*A3					
30			Forecast formula from cell K3			=H3*J3					
31			St Average formula from cell B26			=AVERAGEIFS($G$5:$G$16,$C$5:$C$16,$A26)					

The T_t formula cell reference $B$52 is the Coefficient for the Intercept and $B$53 is the coefficient for the time (t) variable as produced from a DATP regression run (not shown) which used the t values from column A as the independent variable and the T_t values from column J as the dependent variable.

The Forecast (column K) values for Year 5 (rows 19–22) are the car sales forecast values that the dealership needed in order to make decisions for the upcoming year. The Car Sales by Quarter chart shows the forecast values (green line) versus the actual values (red line). Note the green line forecast values extend out through Year 5.

FIGURE 8 Car Sales for Dealership Compared to the Time Series Forecast Values

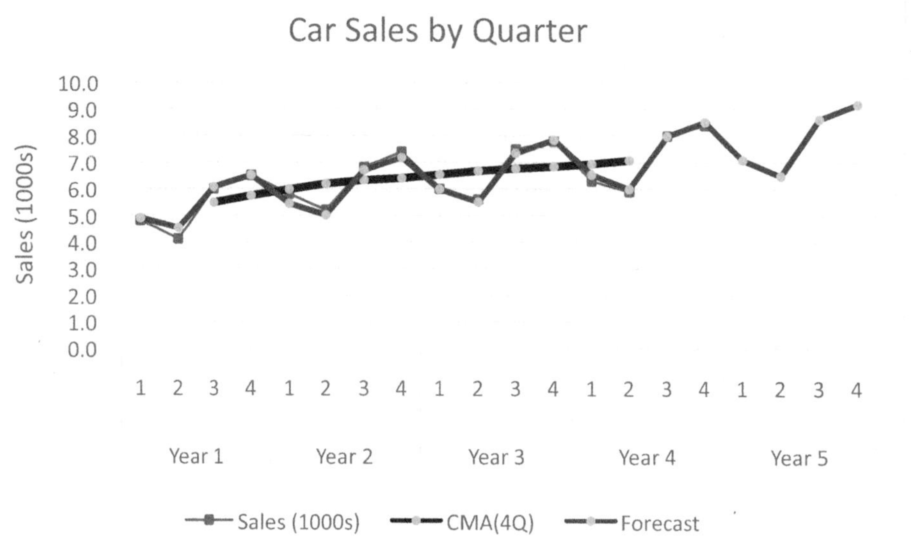

Video Available: Watch the Chapter 7—Time Series video

Reference

Lind, D. A. (2015). *Statistical Techniques in Business & Economics Six.* New York, NY: McGraw-Hill Education.

CHAPTER 8

PRESCRIPTIVE ANALYTICS
Decision Theory

In this chapter, we will explore ways to use data and probabilities to make better business decisions. In previous chapters, we have used **classical statistics**, which focuses on estimating a parameter, such as the population mean, constructing confidence intervals, or hypothesis testing. In this chapter, we will move into **statistical decision theory**, which is concerned with determining which decision from a set of possible decisions is optimal. First, in this chapter, we cover decision theory and the use of payoff matrixes and decision trees. Decision theory provides a framework for choosing between alternative courses of action when the outcomes resulting from the choice is not perfectly known. Every business day presents us with the necessity of making decisions in the face of uncertainty. We must decide on a course of action without knowing the exact consequences that will result from the decision. Decision theory gives us a framework upon which we can use existing data and probabilities of expected outcomes to help maximize expected payoffs and/or minimize expected costs.

There are three components to any decision-making situation or process:

1. The **decision alternatives**, which are under the control of a decision maker
2. The **states of nature**, which are NOT under the control of a decision maker
3. The **payoffs**, which are needed for each combination of decision alternative and state of nature

Video Available: Watch the Chapter 8—Decision Theory video

Payoff Matrix

The expected payoff value is the estimated monetary value for each decision and state of nature combination and in most situations is an implementation of parts or all of the Profit equation.

$$\text{Profit} = \text{Revenue(s)} - \text{Expense(s)}$$

A Payoff Matrix is a two-dimension table listing the expected payoffs for all possible combinations of decision alternatives and states of nature.

TABLE 1 Payoff Matrix for an Investment Decision With Three Options to Buy Stocks (i.e., Kayser Chemicals, Rim Homes, or Texas Electronics) and Two States of Nature (i.e., Bull Market or Bear Market) Example

	A	B	C
1	**Payoff Matrix**		
2	**Decision Alternatives**	**States of Nature**	
3		**Bull Market**	**Bear Market**
4	Kayser Chemicals	$2,400.00	$1,000.00
5	Rim Homes	$2,200.00	$1,100.00
6	Texas Electronics	$1,900.00	$1,150.00

Video Available: Watch the Chapter 8—Payoff Matrix video

The Maximum Expected Monetary Value (EMV) Strategy

The Expected Monetary Value (EMV) is the sum of the expected values times each of their associated probabilities. The Maximum EMV can be used to determine which course of action or decision to pursue. Using the Maximum EMV as a basis for a decision is considered a **balanced approach** since it attempts to balance risks with rewards using probabilities that are based on the likelihood of each state of nature occurring.

$$\text{Calculating the } EMV(A_i) = \sum P(S_i) * V(A_i, S_j)$$
$$\text{Excel Implementaiton: } EMV(A_i) = SUMPRODUCT(P(S_j), V(A_i, S_j))$$

- Let A_i be the ith decision alternative.
- Let $P(S_j)$ be the probability of the jth state of nature.
- Let $V(A_i, S_j)$ be the value of the payoff for the combination of decision alternative A_i and state of nature S_j.
- Let $EMV(A_i)$ be the expected monetary value for the decision alternative A_i.

Using the payoff matrix in Table 2, in column D we calculate the EMV for each decision, then find the maximum EMV in cell D8. After identifying the maximum EMV, we identify which decision has this maximum EMV and base our decision on this maximum value. In this case, we decide to purchase Kayser Chemicals.

TABLE 2 Payoff Matrix With EMV Calculation and Max EMV-Based Decision Example

	A	B	C	D
1	**Payoff Matrix**			
2	**Decision Alternatives**	**States of Nature**		
3		**Bull Market**	**Bear Market**	**EMV**
4	Kayser Chemicals	$2,400.00	$1,000.00	$1,840.00
5	Rim Homes	$2,200.00	$1,100.00	$1,760.00
6	Texas Electronics	$1,900.00	$1,150.00	$1,600.00
7	**Probabilities**			**MAX EMV**
8	EMV formula cell D4	=SUMPRODUCT(B4:C4,$B$7:$C$7)		$1,840.00
9	MAX EMV formula cell D8	=MAX(D4:D6)		
10	MAX EMV Strategy Decision	Purchase Kayser Chemicals		

The MAXIMIN Decision Strategy

The MAXIMIN decision strategy can also be used to determine which course of action or decision to pursue. Using the MAXIMIN strategy as a basis for a decision is considered a **pessimistic approach** since it attempts to minimize risks and does not take probabilities of each state of nature occurring into account. The MAXIMIN strategy is calculated by first finding the minimum expected payoff value for each decision and then finding the maximum value from these minimum expected payoff values. This strategy thus seeks to maximize the expected payoff given that the worst possible state of nature occurs.

TABLE 3 Payoff Matrix With MAXIMIN-Based Decision Example

	A	B	C	D
1	**Payoff Matrix**			
2	**Decision Alternatives**	**States of Nature**		
3		**Bull Market**	**Bear Market**	**MIN**
4	Kayser Chemicals	$2,400.00	$1,000.00	$1,000.00
5	Rim Homes	$2,200.00	$1,100.00	$1,100.00
6	Texas Electronics	$1,900.00	$1,150.00	$1,150.00
7	**Probabilities**	60%	40%	**MAXIMIN**
8	MIN formula from cell D4	=MIN(B4:C4)		$1,150.00
9	MAXIMIN formula cell D8	=MAX(D4:D6)		Texas Electronics
10	MAXIMIN Strategy Decision	Purchase Texas Electronics		

Using the payoff matrix in Table 3, in column D we find the minimum expected payoff value, then find the maximum from those minimum values. After identifying the MAXIMIN, we identify which decision has this maximum value and base our decision on this value. In this case, we decide to purchase Texas Electronics.

The MAXIMAX Decision Strategy

The MAXIMAX decision strategy can also be used to determine which course of action or decision to pursue. Using the MAXIMAX strategy as a basis for a decision is considered an **optimistic approach** since it attempts to maximize returns and does not take probabilities of each state of nature occurring into account. The MAXIMAX strategy is calculated by first finding the maximum expected payoff value for each decision and then finding the maximum value from these maximum expected payoff values. This strategy thus seeks to maximize the expected payoff given that the best possible state of nature occurs.

TABLE 4 Payoff Matrix With MAXIMAX-Based Decision Example

	A	B	C	D
1	Payoff Matrix			
2	Decision (Alternatives)	States of Nature		
3		Bull Market	Bear Market	MAX
4	Kayser Chemicals	$2,400.00	$1,000.00	$2,400.00
5	Rim Homes	$2,200.00	$1,100.00	$2,200.00
6	Texas Electronics	$1,900.00	$1,150.00	$1,900.00
7	Probabilities	60%	40%	MAXIMIN
8	MIN formula from cell D4	=MAX(B4:C4)		$2,400.00
9	MAXIMIN formula cell D8	=MAX(D4:D6)		Kayser Chemicals
10	MAXIMIN Strategy Decision	Purchase Kayser Chemicals		

The Regret Matrix and Expected Opportunity Loss (EOL)

Regret is the loss because the exact state of nature is not known at the time a decision is made. The regret is computed by taking the difference between the optimal decision for each state of nature and the other decision alternatives. The table of the regrets for each decision and state of nature is called a Regret Matrix. The Expected Opportunity Loss (EOL) is the sum of the regrets times each of their associated probabilities. The Minimum EOL can also be used to determine which course of action or decision to pursue. Using the Minimum EOL as a basis for a decision is considered a **balanced approach** since it attempts to balance risks with rewards using probabilities that are based on the likelihood of each state of nature occurring. The Min EOL and Max EMV approach will always lead to the same decision.

$$\textit{Calculating the } EOL(A_i) = \sum P(S_j) * R(A_i, S_j)$$
$$\textit{Excel Implementation: } EOL(A_i) = SUMPRODUCT(P(S_j), R(A_i, S_j))$$

- Let EOL(A_i) refer to the expected opportunity loss for a particular decision alternative
- Let P(S_j) refer to the probability associated with the states of nature j
- Let R(A_i, S_j) refer to the regret or loss for a particular combination of a state of nature and a decision alternative.

TABLE 5 Regret Matrix With EOL Calculation and MIN EOL Decision Example

	A	B	C	D
1	Payoff Matrix			
2	Decision Alternatives	States of Nature		
3		Bull Market	Bear Market	
4	Kayser Chemicals	$2,400.00	$1,000.00	
5	Rim Homes	$2,200.00	$1,100.00	
6	Texas Electronics	$1,900.00	$1,150.00	
7	Probabilities	60%	40%	
8				
9	States of Nature	Bull Market	Bear Market	
10	MAXIMUMS	$2,400.00	$1,150.00	
11	Maximum formula cell B10	=MAX(B4:B6)		
12				
13	Regret Matrix			
14	Decision Alternatives	States of Nature		
15		Bull Market	Bear Market	EOL
16	Kayser Chemicals	$0.00	$150.00	$60.00
17	Rim Homes	$200.00	$50.00	$140.00
18	Texas Electronics	$500.00	$0.00	$300.00
19	Regret formula cell B16	=B$10-B4		MIN EOL
20	EOL formula cell D16	=SUMPRODUCT(B16:C16,$B$7:$C$7)		$60.00
21	MIN EOL formula D20	=MIN(D16:D18)		Kayser Chemicals
22	MIN EOL Strategy Decision	Purchase Kayser Chemicals		

Using the regret matrix in Table 5, in column D we calculate the EOL for each decision, then find the minimum EOL in cell D20. After identifying the minimum EOL, we identify which decision has this minimum EOL and base our decision on this minimum value. In this case, we decide to purchase Kayser Chemicals.

The MINIMAX REGRET Decision Strategy

The MINIMAX REGRET decision strategy can also be used to determine which course of action or decision to pursue. The MINIMAX REGRET strategy attempts to minimize the maximize regret and does not take probabilities of each state of nature occurring into account. The MINIMAX REGRET strategy is calculated by first finding the maximum regret value for each decision and then finding the maximum value from these maximum expected regret values.

TABLE 6 Example Regret Matrix With MINIMAX REGRET Calculation

	A	B	C	D
1	**Payoff Matrix**			
2	**Decision Alternatives**	**States of Nature**		
3		**Bull Market**	**Bear Market**	
4	Kayser Chemicals	$2,400.00	$1,000.00	
5	Rim Homes	$2,200.00	$1,100.00	
6	Texas Electronics	$1,900.00	$1,150.00	
7	**Probabilities**	60%	40%	
8				
9	**States of Nature**	**Bull Market**	**Bear Market**	
10	**MAXIMUMS**	$2,400.00	$1,150.00	
11	Maximum formula cell B10	=MAX(B4:B6)		
12				
13	**Regret Matrix**			
14	**Decision Alternatives**	**States of Nature**		
15		**Bull Market**	**Bear Market**	**MAX**
16	**Kayser Chemicals**	$0.00	$150.00	$150.00
17	**Rim Homes**	$200.00	$50.00	$200.00
18	**Texas Electronics**	$500.00	$0.00	$500.00
19	Regret formula cell B16	=B$10-B4		**MINIMAX REGRET**
20	MAX formula cell D16	=MAX(B16:C16)		$150.00
21	MINIMAX REGRET formula D20	=MIN(D16:D18)		Kayser Chemicals
22	MINIMAX REGRET Strategy Decision	Purchase Kayser Chemicals		

Using the regret matrix in Table 6, in column D we find the maximum regret for each decision, then find the minimum of these maximum regrets in cell D20. After identifying the MINIMAX REGRET, we identify which decision has this MINIMAX REGRET value and base our decision on this value. In this case, we decide to purchase Kayser Chemicals.

Expected Value of Perfect Information (EVPI)

What is the worth of information known in advance before a strategy is employed? Expected Value of Perfect Information *(EVPI)* is the difference between the expected payoff if the state of nature were known and the optimal decision under the conditions of uncertainty. The EVPI is the amount a company would be willing to pay for more accurate information about the states of nature.

The EVPI is calculated taking a SUMPRODUCT of the Probabilities for each State of Nature times the Maximum expected payoff values for each State of Nature and then subtracting out the MAX EMV value.

TABLE 7 Example EVPI Calculation

	A	B	C	D
1	**Payoff Matrix**			
2	**Decision Alternatives**	**States of Nature**		
3		**Bull Market**	**Bear Market**	**EMV**
4	Kayser Chemicals	$2,400.00	$1,000.00	$1,840.00
5	Rim Homes	$2,200.00	$1,100.00	$1,760.00
6	Texas Electronics	$1,900.00	$1,150.00	$1,600.00
7	**Probabilities**	60%	40%	**MAX EMV**
8	**Maximums**	$2,400.00	$1,150.00	$1,840.00
9	**EVPI**	$60.00		
10	EMV formula cell D4	=SUMPRODUCT(B4:C4,$B$7:$C$7)		
11	MAX EMV formula cell D8	=MAX(D4:D6)		
12	Maximums	=MAX(B4:B6)		
13	EVPI formula cell B9	=SUMPRODUCT(B7:C7,B8:C8)-D8		

Video Available: Watch the Chapter 8—Bob Hill video

Decision Trees

A decision **tree** is a graphical representation of all the possible courses of action, events (states of nature), and the consequent possible outcomes.

- A box (decision node) is used to indicate the point at which a decision must be made.
- A circle (event node) indicates a point in the process not under control of decision maker (i.e., an event).

FIGURE 1 Example Decision Tree for an Investment Decision With Three Options to Buy Stocks (i.e., Kayser Chemicals, Rim Homes, or Texas Electronics) and Two States of Nature (i.e., Bull Market or Bear Market)

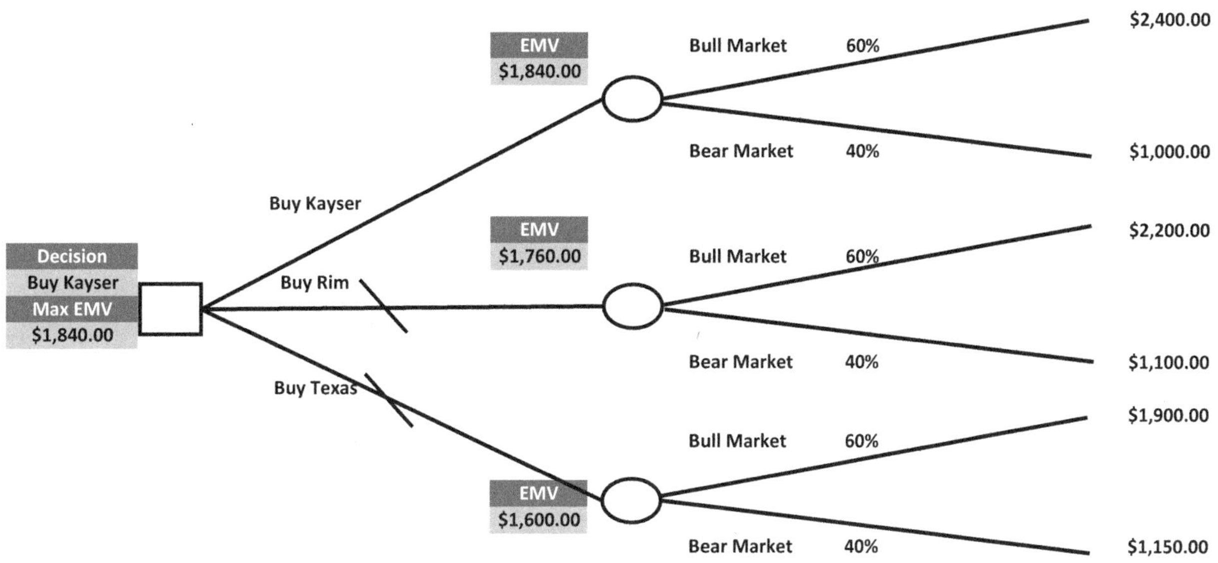

In practice, decision trees are constructed and filled out from left to right and then the expected monetary values are calculated from right to left until the maximum EMV is found.

Video Available: Watch the Chapter 8—Decision Trees video

CHAPTER 9

PRECRIPTIVE ANALYTICS
Optimization

Optimization is a major part of the field of Operations Research. From a business perspective, it normally involves finding a solution that produces the lowest cost, or achieves the highest revenue or profit provided certain constraints. Optimization provides decision-makers the ability to maximize desired factors and to minimize undesired ones. The practice of optimization is restricted by the lack of full information, and the lack of time to evaluate what information is available. In computer modeling of business problems, optimization is usually achieved using linear and nonlinear programming techniques. This chapter will focus solely on linear programming techniques.

Linear programming is an optimization method used to achieve the best outcome for a problem, which involves the following:

- A single objective function which states mathematically what is being maximized or minimized
- Decision variables which represent choices that the decision-maker can control
- Constraints, which are limitations that restrict the decision variables
  - The constraints will be one of three types: ≤, ≥, or =
- A feasible region which is the total solution space that will satisfy all constraints
- A couple of notes:
  - The objective function and constraints must be linear
  - The decision variables will be nonnegative units (*e.g., the manufacturer will not make a negative number of products*)

The objective function is a linear function that is to be optimized (i.e., **profit, revenue, expense, risk, mean square error, etc.**)

A function in which each variable appears in a separate term and is raised to the first power is called a linear function (e.g., (2x4)+(5x6)+(7x3)+… etc.)

A decision variable is a controllable input variable that represents the key decisions a manager must make to achieve an objective.

A constraint is some limitation or requirement that must be satisfied by the solution.

Types of solutions

- **Solution**: any particular combination of decision variables
- **Feasible Solution**: any solution that satisfies all constraints
- **Optimal Solution**: any feasible solution that optimizes the objective function

Examples of Optimization

- Truck routing within a city
- Product shipping from factories to warehouses
- Daily, weekly, monthly production goals
- Inventory management
- Investment management
- Worker scheduling
- Purchasing and pricing

Optimization in Excel is done using the Solver Add-in; to activate the Solver Add-in, click on File > Options > Add-Ins > Go > Solver Add-In >

FIGURE 1 Steps to Follow to Activate Solver in Excel (PC Version 2016)

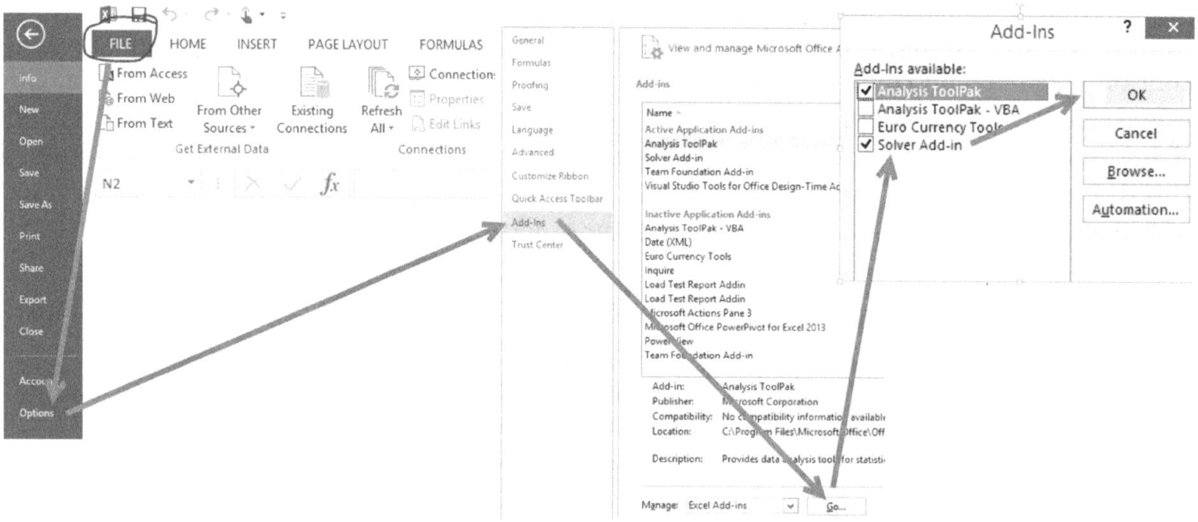

Steps to Build an Optimization Model in Excel

1. Define the decision variables
   * Start by determining how many decision cells you will need
   * It is recommended that you fill in values for your decision variables (e.g., 1's).
2. Determine what you will need to consider in order to implement the objective function
   * With the information you have been given, you should be able to model the objective without considering the constraints
   * Verify your model

3. Write **formulas** so you can check to see that you did not violate **contraints**
   * Formulas will relate to your decision cells
   * Verify your model
4. Implement your model in Solver
   * Remember to check settings

Example Production—Transportation Type Optimization Problem

The SolPro company makes canoe paddles to serve distribution centers in Worchester, Rochester, and Dorchester from existing plants in Battle Creek and Cherry Creek.

Annual demand is expected to increase as projected in the bottom row of the tableau shown in Table 1 below. SolPro is considering locating a plant near the headwaters of Deer Creek. Annual capacity for each plant is shown in the right-hand column of the tableau.

Transportation costs per paddle are shown in the tableau in the small boxes. For example, the cost to ship one paddle from Battle Creek to Worchester is $4.37. What is the optimal transportation costs associated with this allocation problem if demand is to be filled while not exceeding capacity constraints?

TABLE 1 Production—Transportation Type Optimization Solution (Excel)

	A	B	C	D	E	F	G
1	Source	Worchester	Rochester	Dorchester	Total Shipped	Inequality	Capacity
2	Battle Creek	0.0	12000.0	0.0	12000.0	<=	12000
3	Cherry Creek	6000.0	4000.0	0.0	10000.0	<=	10000
4	Deer Creek	0.0	6000.0	12000.0	18000.0	<=	18000
5	Total Received	6000.0	22000.0	12000.0			
6	Inequality	=	=	=			
7	Demand	6000	22000	12000			
8							
9		Transportation Cost per Unit					
10		Destination					
11	Source	Worchester	Rochester	Dorchester			
12	Battle Creek	$4.37	$4.25	$4.89			
13	Cherry Creek	$4.00	$5.00	$5.27			
14	Deer Creek	$4.13	$4.50	$3.75			
15							
16	Objective Function	MIN					
17	Shipping Costs	$167,000.00					
18							
19	Formula Cell B5	=SUM(B2:B4)					
20	Formula Cell E2	=SUM(B2:D2)					
21	Formula Cell B17	=SUMPRODUCT(B2:D4,B12:D14)					

The red-filled cells in the example solution in Table 1 are the decision or "changing" cells that the Solver Add-In changes in order to optimize the objective function (light green fill). The decisions we needed to make in this problem are how many canoe paddles to make at each plant and then how many to ship to each distribution center. The objective is to minimize total shipping costs; shipping costs are based on the number of items shipped from each plant to each distribution center times the corresponding shipping cost per item. The constraints are the total shipped from each plant must be less than or equal to the plant's capacity and the total received at the distribution center must be equal to the number of canoe paddles they required.

FIGURE 2 The Solver Add-in Settings for the Solpro Production–Transportation Model

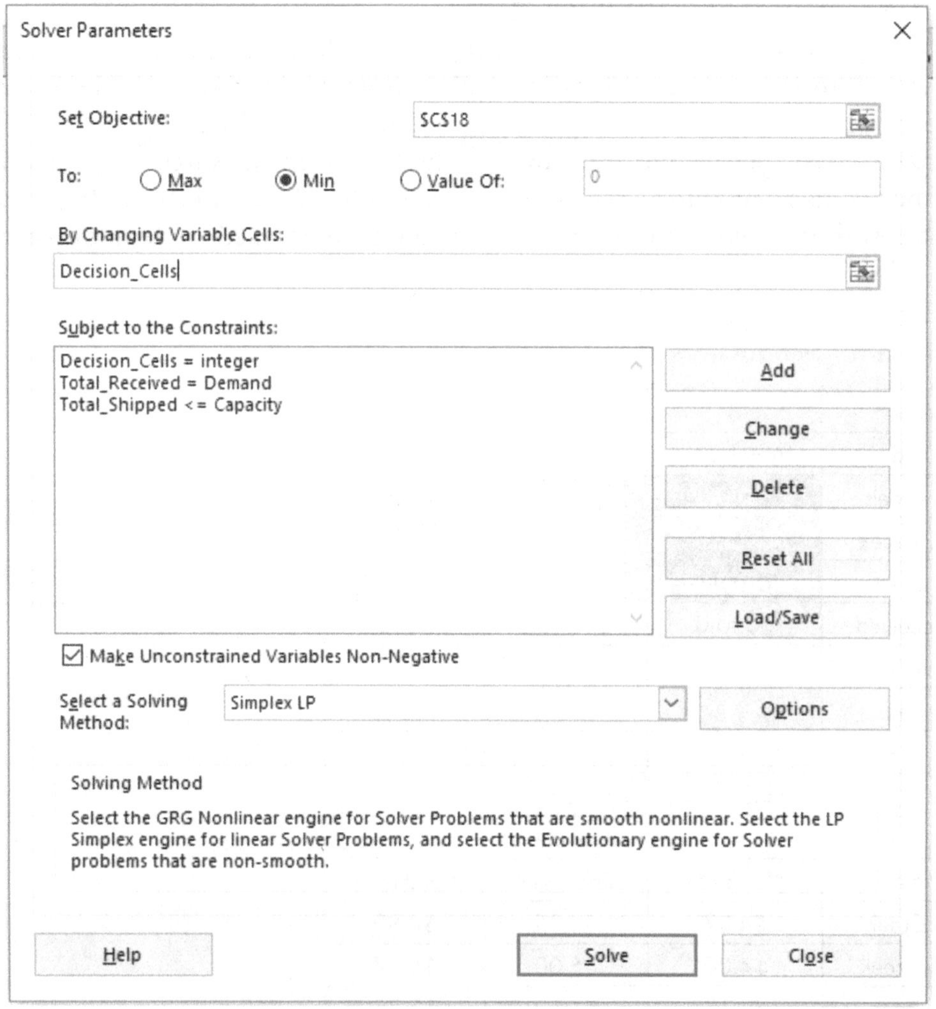

Example Production—Inventory Type Optimization Problem

A medical device company is planning the production of its heart monitor for the next four months. Table 2 shows the regular and overtime production cost per unit, the maximum regular time production, the maximum overtime production, and the demand for each month. Production each month can be either regular time or overtime (or both). Develop a model to determine the number of units to be produced on regular time and overtime to minimize total cost during the next four months.

TABLE 2 Starting Information for Heart Monitor Optimization Problem

Starting Inventory = 50 units	January	February	March	April
Regular Time Production Cost per Unit	$95.00	$95.00	$95.00	$95.00
Overtime Production Cost per Unit	$145.00	$145.00	$145.00	$145.00
Maximum Regular Time Production	210	210	210	210
Maximum Overtime Production	180	180	180	180
Minimum Safety Stock	40	40	40	40
Inventory Holding Cost per Unit	$30.00	$30.00	$30.00	$30.00

TABLE 3 Production—Inventory Type Optimization Solution (Excel)

	A	B	C	D	E
1		January	February	March	April
2	Regular Time Production	210.0	210.0	210.0	210.0
3	Overtime Production	62.0	10.0	152.0	60.0
4	Regular Time Production Cost per Unit	$95.00	$95.00	$95.00	$95.00
5	Overtime Production Cost per Unit	$145.00	$145.00	$145.00	$145.00
6	Beginning Inventory	50	40	40	40
7	Total Production	272	220	362	270
8	Demand	282	220	362	270
9	Ending Inventory	40	40	40	40
10	Average Inventory	45	40	40	40
11	Inventory Holding Cost per Unit	$30.00	$30.00	$30.00	$30.00
12					
13	Copy 1 Regular Time Production	210	210	210	210
14	Inequality	<=	<=	<=	<=
15	Maximum Regular Time Production	210	210	210	210
16					
17	Copy 1 Overtime Production	62	10	152	60
18	Inequality	<=	<=	<=	<=
19	Maximum Overtime Production	180	180	180	180
20					
21	Copy 1 Ending Inventory	40	40	40	40
22	Inequality	>=	>=	>=	>=
23	Minimum Safety Stock	40	40	40	40
24					
25	Regular Time Production Cost	$79,800.00			
26	Overtime Production Cost	$41,180.00			
27	Inventory Cost	$4,950.00			
28	Objective Function	MIN			
29	Total Cost	$125,930.00			
30					
31	Beginning Inventory = Previous Month Ending Inventory				
32	Total Production = Regular Time + Overtime Production				
33	Ending Inventory = Beginning Inventory + Total Production - Demand				
34	Average Inventory = (Beginning Inventory + Ending Inventory)/2				
35	Regular Time Production Cost	=SUMPRODUCT(B2:E2,B4:E4)			
36	Overtime Production Cost	=SUMPRODUCT(B3:E3,B5:E5)			
37	Inventory Cost	=SUMPRODUCT(B10:E10,B11:E11)			
38	Total Cost	=B25+B26+B27			

The red-filled cells in the example solution in Table 3 are the decision or "changing" cells that the Solver Add-In changes in order to optimize the objective function (light green fill). The decisions we needed to make in this problem are how many heart monitors to make during regular time and during overtime. The objective is to minimize the total costs; total costs include regular time production costs, overtime production costs, and inventory costs. The constraints are the maximum regular time production, the maximum overtime production, and the minimum safety stock. We also need to have an integer constraint to ensure that the solution does not include the production of partial heart monitors.

FIGURE 3 The Solver Add-In Settings for the Heart Monitors Production-Inventory Model

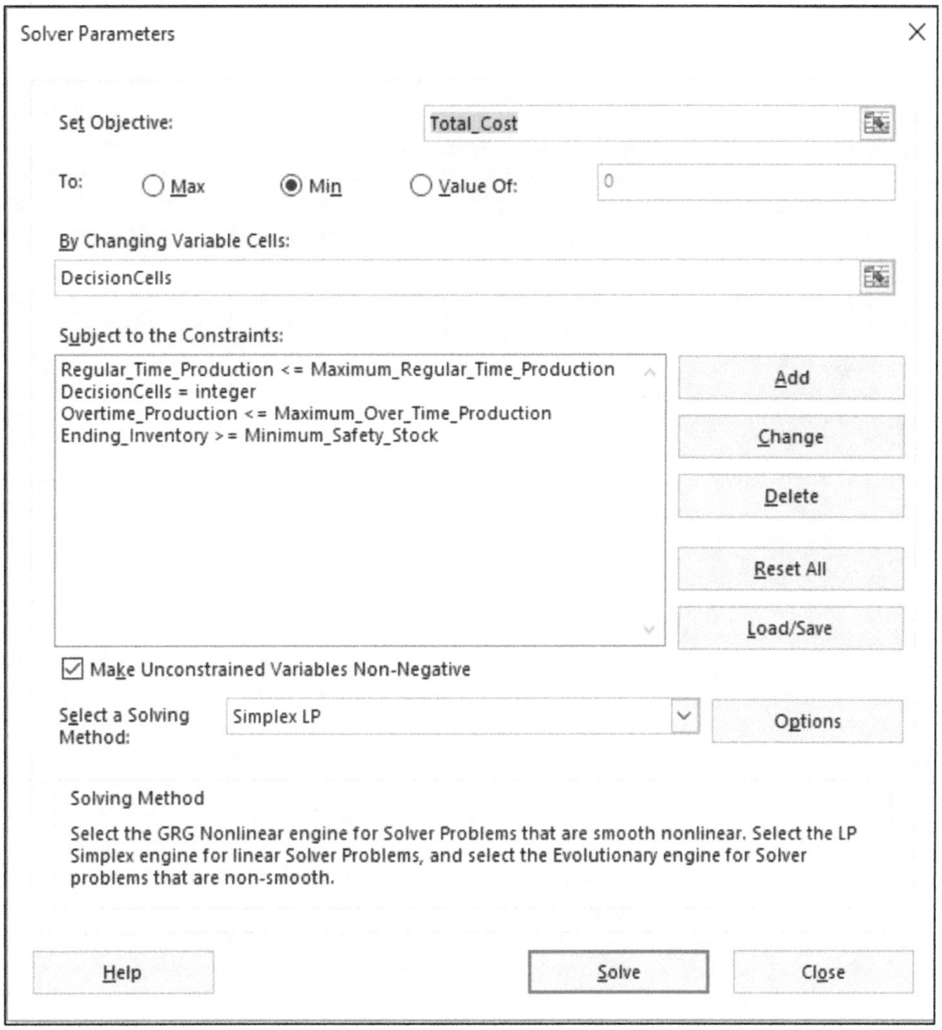

INDEX

D

E